AF317000

Ceremonies and Liturgy of the A.S.A.

By +Mike Bais, Priest and Bishop within the A.S.A,
founder of Circle of Avalon - School of the Soul
(Kabbalah and Western Mystery Tradition)

First edition 2024

Copyright © Mike Bais 2024

All liturgy forthcoming out of the tradition and lineage of the A.S.A.
and preserved and transmitted by +Mike Bais (first attending Priest
and Bishop in the Netherlands) in service of the Way of Christ.
The moral right of the author has been asserted.

All rights reserved

No part of this book may be reproduced, stored in a retrieval system,
or transmitted in any form or by any means without prior permission
in writing of the publisher, nor be circulated in any form of
binding or cover, other than that in which it is published and without
a similar condition including this condition being imposed on
the subsequent purchaser.

Publisher: Circle of Avalon Books in cooperation with Ingram Spark
ISBN: 9789082999099

Contact the author: mike@circleofavalon.nl

Table of contents

Part 1 Holy Mass

The Holy Mass (original form)

A.S.A. APOSTOLIC SUCCESSION OF ARIMATHEA

Opening

Stillness, invocation, procession and chant towards the altar

Invocation

Priest: This is the Day God has made

Congregation: Let us rejoice and be glad

Priest: I will go up to the Altar of God

Congregation: Even unto the God of my Joy and Gladness

Priest: Send forth Thy Light and Thy Truth
That they may lead me, and bring me unto Thy Holy Hill,
And to Thy Dwelling Place

Congregation: And I will go up to the Altar of God, even unto
the God of my Joy and Gladness

Priest: In the Name of God, the Creator, the ✠ Redeemer and
the Transforming Spirit

Congregation: Amen

Asperges

(Priest performs Aspergil - three times self, three times the altar and
three times the congregation)

Priest: All Encompassing One, Who ceaselessly creates and sustains
the fabric of the Universe; send forth Your Holy and Beloved Angels,
To guard, encourage, protect and teach all who dwell within this place.

In Your strength O God, do we command all adverse powers,
to wither into nothingness, that they shall not abide, and that our
temples ☥ within, and our temples ☥ without, may emerge as strong,
pure vessels, to contain the Eternal Mystery, as it unfolds on earth

Congregation: Amen

Lighting of the Four Candles & Invoking the Four Archangels

Priest: I will kindle my fire this Day (Night),
In the Presence of the Four Archangels of Heaven,
In the Presence of Raphael, regent of the Air,
In Presence of Michael, regent of the Fire,
In Presence of Gabriel, regent of the Waters,
In Presence of Uriel, regent of the Earth,

Without malice, without jealousy,
Without envy, without fear,
Without terror of anyone under the sun

Congregation: God, Kindle Thou in my heart within,
A flame of love to my neighbour,
To my foe, to my friend, to my kindred and all,
To the brave, to the knave, to the thrall,
The Blessings of Heaven be upon us,
From the lowliest creature that liveth,
To the Name that is highest of all,
Amen

Purification & First Censing

Priest: Purify this place O God, and make of us One Body,
Growing into the fullness of Christ,
A Temple of Living Stones, through which Infinite Life may flow,
Let the Angels and Archangels join us in this Work of transforming
the Earth

Addressing penitential rite

Priest: My companions, to prepare ourselves to receive and celebrate
the Sacred Mysteries, let us make our confession before God.
Open yourself before the Holy One and become available to
the Source who has given Its Life for you. Emphata!

Congregation: Create in me a clean heart. O forgiving Love,
And renew a right Spirit within me,
Here is my body, I cast it down before you,
Heal its imperfections with your perfection and make me whole
Here is my mind, I spread it out before you,
Forgive my foolishness and ignorance with Your Bright Wisdom,
Here is my heart, it is Yours alone, forgive its restless wanderings
from You,
Here is my life, I offer it unto You, do with me as You will,
forgive me,
Together with Yourself, restore unto me, the Joy of Your Salvation,
That I may awake in Your Likeness and be satisfied,
Through Christ, the Indwelling Light, Amen

Absolution

Priest: The Mercy and Grace of God be upon you ✙ will forgive all
your sins and bring us to Eternal Light

Congregation: Amen

KYRIE

KYRIE ELEISON
KYRIE ELEISON
KYRIE ELEISON
CHRISTE ELEISON
CHRISTE ELEISON
CHRISTE ELEISON
KYRIE ELEISON
KYRIE ELEISON
KYRIE ELEISON

Gloria

Priest: Glory be to God, the Inmost and Most Highest

Congregation: And Peace to its people on earth. Almighty God our
Father - Mother,
We worship You, we give You thanks, we praise You for your Glory,
Christ, all Redeeming One, Son of the Great Light, Help and Heal
us all. You are seated at the Right Hand of the Father, receive
our prayer,
For You are the Chief among the Holy Ones,
You are the Anointed One,
The Beloved Child, who with the Holy Spirit,
Art one in the ✠ Glory of God. Amen.

Collect

Priest: The Holy One be with you

Congregation: And also with you

Priest: Let us pray

Congregation: O God the Giver of all gifts,
We praise You, the Source of all we have and are,
You shelter us beneath the shadow of Your Wings,
And search into the depths of our hearts,
Your Light is strong, your Love is here,
Remove the blindness that cannot know you, and relieve the fear that
would hide us from Your Sight,
Touched by Your hand, our world is Holy,
Open our eyes to see Your Hand at work in the Splendor of Creation,
and the beauty of human life,
Draw us beyond the limits, which this world imposes to the life
where Your Spirit makes all life complete,
We ask this through Your Son the Christ, Your Child,
Who lives and reigns with You and the Holy Spirit,
One God, forever and ever. Amen

Liturgy of the word (readings)

Priest: The first reading is from (appropriate scripture or text follows)

Priest: This is the Word of God, the Logos incarnate

Congregation: Thanks be to God

Gradual

Priest: Whoever loves Wisdom, loves life, and they that seek her
early, shall be filled with joy. Teach me, O God, the Path to Your
Mystery, and I shall keep it unto the end. Give me understanding
and I shall keep Your Law, I shall keep it with my whole my heart
For the Path of the Just is as the Shining Light, shining more
and more unto that perfect day

Second reading of the Gospel

Invocation: Cleanse my heart and my lips O Most High, Who by
the Hand of Your Angel-Seraph, did cleanse the lips of your Prophets
with that of a burning coal from Your Altar. And in Your loving -
kindness, purify me, that I may proclaim the Holy Gospel

Priest: May the Divine be in your ♱ heart and on your ♱ lips, that
through your heart the Love of God may shine forth and your mouth
may manifest Its Power. Amen

Priest or altar servant: The Holy One be with you

Congregation: And also with you

Priest: This is a reading from the Holy scriptures according to……
(reading)

Priest: This is the Good News according to……

Congregation: Praise to You O Christ

Sermon (meditation)

Credo

Congregation:
I Believe in God the Divine Mystery, beyond all definition and all
rational understanding, the Heart of all that ever existed, that exists
now and ever will exist

I Believe in Christ, Messenger of God's Word, Bringer of Gods
Healing,
Heart of Gods Compassion, Bright Star in the Firmament, of Gods
Prophets, Mystics and Saints

I Believe in the Holy Spirit, the Life of God that is our Innermost
Life, the Breath of God moving in our Being, the Depth of God
Living in each of us

I Believe that I am called to be Christ's Twin, allowing myself to
be a vehicle of God's Love, a Source of Gods Wisdom and Truth,
and an instrument of Gods Peace in the World

I Believe that Gods Reign is here and now, stretched out all around
us for those with eyes to see it, hearts to receive it and hands to make
it happen

I Believe in the community of God seekers, in all religions, the works
of the prophets, mystics and saints, and those just beginning their
Spiritual Journey

I Believe in a future on this earth, when all will be God-centred
and God conscious, when we will learn to live in Peace and Love,
in the fellowship of brothers and sisters

I Believe that in death life is changed, not taken away and that we
will always go, from step to step in Gods Life, Gods Love and Gods
Glory for All Eternity. Amen. Amen. Amen.

Prayers of the Faithful

Priest: My companions, let us call to mind God's many Blessings and ask to hear the prayers which are inspired to ask

Priest: For all of us gathered in this Holy place, in faith, reverence and love of God, that we may offer an acceptable sacrifice
We pray to the Holy One:

Congregation: Beloved One hear our prayer

Priest: For God's Holy Church, within and without and every place of worship at this very moment, and all its devotees and those who lead them. That Christ guides and protect them
We pray to the Holy One:

Congregation: Beloved One hear our prayer

Priest: For all our brothers and sisters in need, that the Holy One guides and assist them all
We pray to the Holy One:

Congregation: Beloved One hear our prayer

Priest: For all the peoples of the world, that God unites them in Peace, Love and Harmony
We pray to the Holy One:

Congregation: Beloved One hear our prayer

Priest: For those who serve us in public office and those entrusted with the common good
We pray to the Holy One:

Congregation: Beloved One hear our prayer

Priest: For those who are in sickness or in suffering, especially for those souls who we now name before Thee (read names)
We pray to the Holy One:

Congregation: Beloved One hear our prayer

Priest: For all the departed and those who mourn them. Especially those who we now name before Thee (read names)
We pray to the Holy One:

Congregation: Beloved One hear our prayer

Priest: And for any special intentions that you may have, said in silent prayer
(Pause)...... we pray to the Holy One:

Congregation: Beloved One hear our prayer

Priest: Now let us call upon our Heavenly Mother, asking Her to unite our prayers with Hers, as we say:

Congregation: Hail Mary full of Grace, the Beloved and Holy One is with Thee. Blessed art Thou amongst women, and Blessed is the Fruit of thy Womb. Holy Mary, Mother of God, pray for us now, and at the hour of our victory, over sin, disease and death. Amen

Sign of Peace

Priest: My companions, we have confessed our sins and we have been forgiven; Christ the Compassionate King, binds us with a bond of Love that cannot be broken. Therefore in the Name of the Logos ever present ever saying: "Peace I leave with you, my Peace I give unto you; not as the world gives do I give it unto you"

Priest: The Peace of Christ be with you always

Congregation: And also with you

Presentation of the Gifts

(Priest lifts Shroud from the Grail and Paten)

Priest: Leave the mortal and the temporal to the realm of the world,
for they are as dust and ash, while I am Immortal and Eternal
amongst you. Behold Me as I Am and behold your own face within
Me (presentation Shroud and bell sounds)

Priest: Most Holy One, accept that of which by the nature of
this planet we are composed, and in our great gratitude, we offer
this Bread unto You, as we likewise offer ourselves

Congregation: On this paten O Christ with this Bread, we place all
the creative actions of the people of the earth; their aspirations,
their joy, their achievements and their work

Priest: Blessed are You, God of all Creation, through Your Goodness
we have this Bread to offer, which earth has given and human hands
have made
It will become for us, our ✢ Bread of Life

Congregation: Blessed be God forever

Priest: As your Spirit would move the heart of every being,
So we move water within this wine, and they shall move as one

Priest: We adore you O God, and offer unto You this water and wine,
as we offer that which gives us life. From You have we come and
unto You we shall return

Congregation: Into our Chalice with this wine, we pour the sorrows,
the pain and the suffering of all your creation. Into this offering
of the world, we would gather those closest to us, those whose lives
are bound up with our own

Priest: Blessed are You God of all creation, through Your Goodness we
have this Wine to offer; fruit of the vine and work of human hands.

It will become for us our ✚ Spiritual Drink

Congregation: Blessed be God forever

Sign of Bondage

Congregation: With these we unite those more distant and less
familiar to us,
The great multitude of humanity, scattered over every part
of the globe,

In deepest sympathy and understanding, we unite ourselves,
With the ceaseless pilgrimage of humanity; past, present and future,
With all its joys and sorrows, its hopes and fears, that we may
be one with them all

We would draw into this offering every form of life; animals, trees,
flowers and fruits, rocks and fire, wind and water, and the very fabric
of the earth itself. We offer ourselves, all that we have and all
that we are,
Let all Existence be now placed on our altar, that we may raise
it up to Thee.

Second Censing

(Priest performs censing of the offerings and the congregation)

Priest: Receive O Source of Life, this Your manifold Creation,
in all its Light and all its Darkness

Congregation: Amen

Lavabo

Priest: I will wash my hands in innocence O God and so I will go to
Your Altar and offer Your Mystery to those who wish to receive

Orate Fratres

Priest: Pray my companions, that our sacrifice may be acceptable
to God

Congregation: May God accept this sacrifice at your hands
and sanctify our lives in Holy Service

Prayer over the gifts

Priest: Most Holy and Beloved One, by these Holy Gifts we offer,
make ✙ Holy those who gather in Your Name. May we who share
this Sacrament, experience the Life and Power it promises and enter
your Presence.

Congregation: Amen

Sursum Corda

Priest: The Holy One be with you
Congregation: And also with you

Priest: Lift up your hearts
Congregation: We lift them up to the Most High

Priest: Let us give thanks to God
Congregation: It is right to give thanks and praise

Preface

Congregation: O Holy One of Blessing, God of all Being
We do well always and everywhere to give You thanks
You have no need of our praise, yet our desire to thank You is itself
Your Gift
Our prayer of thanksgiving adds nothing to Your Greatness,
but makes us to grow in Your Grace
You give us Your Holy Spirit, the Comforter, to help us always with
Her Power, so that with loving trust, we may turn to You in all our
troubles and give You thanks in all our joys

Priest: Source of life and goodness, you have created all things,
To fill Your creatures with every Blessing, and lead all to the Joyful
Vision of Your Light. Countless Hosts of Angels, stand before You,
to do Your Will.
They look upon You, and praise You night and day.

United with them, with Angels and Archangels, with Thrones,
Dominations, Princedoms, Virtues and Powers, with Cherubim,
Seraphim and Ashim,
And in the Name of every creature under Heaven,
We too praise Your Glory as we say:

Sanctus

Congregation: Holy! Holy! Holy! God of Power and Might
Heaven and earth are full of Your Glory
Hosanna in the Highest
Blessed are those who come in the Name of the Holy One
Hosanna in the Highest

Canon of the Mass

Priest: Holy One, You are Holy indeed, the Fountain of all Holiness,
As one family we gather around Your Table,
Here is the Sacrifice of Christ offered in Mystery

Here is prepared the Sacred Table, at which Your children,
Are nourished by the Body of Christ,
Here Your people drink from the Living Spirit,
The Stream of Living Water, that flows from the Stone of Christ
Loving Creator, we bring You all these gifts of Bread ✠ and Wine ✠
And ourselves as a living sacrifice

Let Your Spirit descend upon these gifts, to make them Holy,
Sanctify them, that they may become,
The Body ✠ and Blood ✠ of Christ,
Who has willed us to make this Eucharist

Consecration

Priest: The Day before He suffered He took Bread into His
Sacred Hands,
And with His Eyes lifted up to Heaven, He gave You thanks
and praise.
He broke and ✠ blessed the Bread, giving it unto His disciples,
saying:

"Take and eat this all of you, for:

This is my Body"

Priest: When supper was ended, He took this Cup into His
Sacred Hands,
Again He gave You thanks and praise. He blessed ✠ the Cup,
and gave it unto His disciples saying:

"Take and drink this all of you, for:

This is the Cup of My Blood"

Whenever you do these things I AM is present among you

Affirmation

Congregation: Thee we adore O Hidden Splendour Thee
Who in Thy Sacrament dost deign to be
We worship Thee beneath this earthly veil
And here Thy Presence we devoutly hail

Priest: Most Holy One, we celebrate the Mystery of Christ,
we Your people and ministers, recall the incarnation and Passion,
the triumphant resurrection from the dead and the ascension into
Your Glory
And from the many gifts You have given us, we offer to You,
God of Glory and Majesty, this Holy and Perfect Sacrifice:
The Bread ✠ of Life
And the Cup of ✠ Eternal Salvation

Congregation: Look with favour on these offerings and accept
them as once you accepted the gifts of Abraham and Sarah,
our parents in Faith, and the Wine and Bread offered by Your
High-Priest, Melchizedek.

Priest: Almighty God, we pray that Your Angel may take this
Sacrifice to Your altar on High. There to be offered by those,
Who as the Eternal High Priest, forever offer themselves as
the Eternal Sacrifice,
And as Christ willed that the Heavenly Sacrifice shall be mirrored
here on earth, so that Your people may be united more closely to You,
We pray for Your servants, Who minister at this altar,
That by celebrating these Mysteries, of the Divine Body ✚
and Blood ✚
They may be filled ✚ with Your Mighty Power and Blessing

Priest: Loving God, we call You Father, but You are the fountain of
Motherhood, male and female You created us, in Your own image
and likeness,
May all people come to know, that in You, there is no male or female,
No distinction between race, class or colour, for we are all one
within You

Congregation: Through Christ, You give us all these Gifts
You fill them with Life and Goodness
You Bless them and make them Holy

Minor Elevation

Priest: By ✚ Him, with ✚ Him, and in ✚ Him,
In the Unity of the Holy Spirit,
All Glory and Honour is Yours Almighty God
Forever and ever

Congregation: Amen

Communion Rite & Christ's Prayer

Congregation: Our Father Who art in Heaven, Hallowed be
Thy Name, Thy Kingdom come, Thy Will be done, on earth
as it is in Heaven,
Give us this day our daily bread and forgive us our trespasses,
As we forgive those who trespass against us, and lead us not into
temptation, but deliver us from evil,
For Thee ✤ is the Kingdom, and the Power and the Glory,
Forever and ever. Amen

Alternative Prayer

Congregation: Oh Thou, from Whom the Breath of Life comes,
Who fills all realms of sound, light and vibration,
May Your Light be known in my utmost Holiest of Being
Your Heavenly Domain approaches, let Your Will come true,
on earth as it is in Heaven,
Give us Wisdom for our daily need and detach the fetters of our
faults that bind us, like we let go the guilt of others,
And let us not be lost in worldly things, but let us be free from
what keeps us from our true purpose,
From You comes the all-working Will, the Lively Strength to act,
the Song that Beautifies all, and renews itself from age to age,
Sealed in Love, Faith and Truth. Amen, Amen, Amen.

Veneration of Saints

Priest: Here we give praise to those channels of Your grace,
the Just Ones made perfect: Enoch, Melchizedek, Yahushua-Christ,
Joseph of Arimathea, Maria Magdalena, Nicodemus,
John the Beloved, Teresa of Avila, Martha of Bethany, Bartholomew,
Jacob Boehme, Nicodemus, Thomas Aquinas, Meister Eckhart, ...
and any other saints or teachers that you wish to venerate (silence)....

And we ✤ join with them before Your Great White Throne,
from which flows Infinite Love, Light and Blessing, through all the
worlds that You have made

Fraction

Priest: O Son of God, You show Yourself this day upon countless
altars, yet, truly remain one and indivisible,
In token of Your great Sacrifice, we break (breaking of the Host) this,
Your Body…
And in token of Your Triumph over ✠ death, and the oneness of Your ✠
Spirit and Body, and Your Glorious ✠ Resurrection, we unite this
Your Body, with this Your Blood (unite)
Praying that by this action ordained from old, they may be for us,
and for all the world, a channel of Grace and of Life Eternal.

Congregation: Amen

Agnus Dei

Priest: Lamb of God, slain from the Foundation of the world
Congregation: Help and Heal us all

Priest: Lamb of God, slain from the Foundation of the world
Congregation: Help and Heal us all

Priest: Lamb of God, slain from the Foundation of the world
Congregation: Grant us Peace

Priest: This is the Lamb of God slain from the Foundation of
the world, happy are those who take place at His Supper

Congregation: Christ our Passover is sacrificed for us, therefore
let us keep the feast,
As You gave Your Body and Blood, so I offer myself wholly unto
You. My body and my blood, to transform as You Will, that Your
Mystery is completed within me ✠

Communion

(Priest receives and gives out communion)

Priest:
The Body of Christ ✠ and the Bread of Angels,
The Blood of Christ ✠ and the Grail of Eternal Life

Post communion prayer

Priest: I have eaten Your Sacred Body, no darkness will take me,
I have looked upon it, now my eyes see Your Wonders,
I have not been a stranger to Your Mysteries,
I am never separated from You ✠

Conclusion

Priest: let us pray

Congregation: Under the veil of earthly things, now we are in
communion with the Holy Spirit. With open face we behold Christ,
and being made anew, like unto its own Glorious Body, may we
abide in Your Presence always O God, and serve You night and day.
Amen

Priest: The Mystery is complete and the rite has ended and
the Blessed Archangels depart in Joy and Peace

All: We give thanks to all the Holy Angels of Heaven and to God
Who send them

Priest: The Blessings of God the Creator, the Redeemer ✠ and
the Transforming Spirit. Amen

Priest: Ite Missa Est

Congregation: Deo Gratias

The Holy Mass (shorter form)

A.S.A. APOSTOLIC SUCCESSION OF ARIMATHEA

Opening: (stillness, invocation, procession and chant to the altar)

Priest and clergy enter and stand before the altar.
A moment of silence…

Priest: In the Name of God, the Creator, the + Redeemer and
the Transforming Spirit

Congregation: Amen

(Priest performs Aspergil - three times self, three times the altar and
three times the congregation)
Priest: Cleanse me with Hyssop O God and make me whiter than snow

Priest: All Encompassing One, Who ceaselessly creates and sustains,
The fabric of the Universe, send forth Your Holy and beloved Angels,
To guard, encourage, protect and teach all who dwell within
this place.
In Your strength O God, do we command all adverse powers,
to wither into nothingness, that they shall not abide,
And that our temples + within, and our temples + without,
May emerge as strong, pure vessels,
To contain the Eternal Mystery, as it unfolds on earth

Lighting of the Four candles

Priest: I will kindle my fire this day / night,
In the Presence of the four Archangels of Heaven;
In the Presence of Raphael, regent of the Air,
In the Presence of Michael, regent of the Fire
In Presence of Gabriel, regent of the Waters
In Presence of Uriel, regent of the Earth,

Without malice, without jealousy,
Without envy, without fear,
Without terror of anyone under the sun

Congregation: God, Kindle Thou in my heart within,
A flame of love to my neighbour,
To my foe, to my friend, to my kindred and all,
To the brave, to the knave, to the thrall,
The blessings of Heaven be upon us,
From the lowliest creature that liveth,
To the Name that is highest of all,
Amen

Purification

(First censing & invocation of the Angel of Christ)

Priest: Purify this place O God, and make of us One Body,
Growing into the Fullness of Christ,
A Temple of Living Stones, through which Infinite Life may flow,
Let the Angels and Archangels join us in this Work of transforming
the earth

Addressing penitential rite

Priest: My companions, to prepare ourselves to receive and celebrate
the Sacred Mysteries, let us make our confession before God

All: Create in me a clean heart. O forgiving Love,
And renew a right Spirit within me,
Here is my body, I cast it down before you,
Heal its imperfections with your perfection and make me whole.
Here is my mind, I spread it out before you,
Forgive my foolishness and ignorance with Your bright wisdom.
Here is my heart, it is Yours alone,
Forgive its restless wanderings from You.
Here is my life, I offer it unto You,
Do with me as You will, forgive me,
Together with yourself, restore unto me, the joy of Your Salvation,

That I may awake in Your likeness and be satisfied,
Through Christ, the Indwelling Light. Amen

Absolution

Priest: The Mercy and Grace of the Son of Light be upon you ✞ will
forgive all your sins and bring us to Eternal Light

Congregation: Amen

Collect

Priest: The Holy One be with you

Congregation: And also with you

Priest: Let us pray

All: O God the Giver of all gifts,
We praise You, the Source of all we have and are.
You shelter us beneath the shadow of Your Wings,
And search into the depths of our hearts,
Your Light is strong, your Love is here,
Remove the blindness that cannot know you, and relieve the fear
that would hide us from Your Sight.
Touched by Your hand, our world is Holy,

Open our eyes to see Your Hand at work in the splendor of creation,
and the beauty of human life.
Draw us beyond the limits, which this world imposes,
To the life where Your Spirit makes all life complete.
We ask this through Your Son the Christ, Your Child,
Who lives and reigns with You and the Holy Spirit,
One God, forever and ever
Amen

Sign of Peace

Priest: My companions, we have confessed our sins and we have
been forgiven;
Christ the Compassionate King, binds us with a bond of Love that
cannot be broken.
Therefore in the Name of the Logos ever present ever saying:
"Peace I leave with you, my Peace I give unto you, not as the world
gives do I give it unto you"

The Peace of Christ be always with you

Congregation: And also with you

Presentation of the Gifts

(Priest lifts Shroud from the Grail and Paten)

Priest: Leave the mortal and the temporal to the realm of the world,
for they are as dust and ash, while I am Immortal and Eternal
amongst you. Behold Me as I Am and behold your own face within
Me (presentation Shroud)

Priest: Most Holy One, accept that of which by the nature of
this planet we are composed, and in our great gratitude, we offer
this Bread unto You, as we likewise offer ourselves.

Congregation: On this paten Oh Christ, with this Bread, we place all
the creative actions of the peoples of the earth, their aspirations, their
joy, their achievements and their work.

Priest: Blessed are You, God of all Creation. Through Your Goodness
we have this Bread to offer, which earth has given and human hands
have made.
It will become for us, our + Bread of Life.

Congregation: Blessed be God forever

Priest: As your Spirit would move the heart of every being,
Now we move Water within this Wine, and they shall move as one.

Priest: We adore you O God, and offer unto You this Water and
Wine, as we offer that which gives us life. From You have we come
and unto You shall we return.

Congregation: Into our Chalice with this Wine, we pour the sorrows,
the pain and the suffering of all your creation. Into this offering of
the world, we would gather those closest to us, those whose lives are
bound up with our own.

Priest: Blessed are You God of all Creation, through Your Goodness
we have this Wine to offer, Fruit of the Vine and work of
human hands.
It will become for us our + Spiritual drink

Congregation: Blessed be God forever

Prayer over the gifts

Priest: Most Holy One, by these Holy Gifts we offer, make + Holy
those who gather in Your Name. May we who share this Sacrament,
experience the life and power it promises and enter Your Presence.

Congregation: Amen

Sursum Corda

Priest: The Holy One be with you
Congregation: And also with you

Priest: Lift up your hearts
Congregation: We lift them up to the Most High

Priest: Let us give thanks to God
Congregation: It is right to give thanks and praise

Preface

Congregation: O Holy One of Blessing, God of all Being
We do well always and everywhere to give you thanks.
You have no need of our praise, yet our desire to thank you is itself
your gift.
Our prayer of thanksgiving adds nothing to Your greatness,
but makes us to grow in Your Grace.
You give us Your Holy Spirit, the Comforter, to help us always with
Her Power, so that with loving trust, we may turn to You in all our
troubles and give You thanks in all our joys

Priest: Source of life and goodness, You have created all things,
To fill Your creatures with every Blessing, and lead all to the joyful
vision of Your Light. Countless hosts of Angels, stand before You,
to do Your Will.
They look upon You, and praise You night and day.
United with them; with Angels and Archangels, with Thrones,
dominations, Princedoms, Virtues and Powers,
With Cherubim, Seraphim and Ashim,
And in the Name of every creature under Heaven,
We too praise Your Glory as we say:

Sanctus

Congregation: Holy! Holy! Holy! God of Power and Might
Heaven and earth are full of Your Glory
Hosanna in the Highest.
Blessed are those who come in the Name of the Holy One
Hosanna in the Highest

Canon of the Mass

Priest: God, You are Holy indeed, the Fountain of all Holiness,
As one family we gather around Your Table,
Here is the Sacrifice of Christ offered in mystery

Here is prepared the Sacred Table, at which Your children,
Are nourished by the Body of Christ,

Here Your people drink from the Living Spirit,
The stream of living water, that flows from the Stone of Christ.
Loving Creator, we bring You all these gifts of Bread + and Wine +
and ourselves as a Living Sacrifice
Let Your Spirit descend upon these Gifts and make them Holy,
Sanctify them, that they may become,
The Body + and Blood + of Christ,
Who has willed us to make this Eucharist

Consecration

Priest: The day before He suffered He took Bread into
His Sacred Hands,
And with His Eyes lifted up to Heaven, He gave You thanks
and praise.
He broke and + blessed the Bread, giving it unto
His disciples, saying:

"Take and eat this all of you, for this is My Body"

When supper was ended, He took this Cup into His Sacred Hands,
Again He gave You thanks and praise. He blessed + the Cup,
and gave it unto His disciples saying:

"Take and drink this all of you, for this is the Cup of My Blood"

Whenever you do these things I AM is present among you!

Affirmation

Congregation: Thee we adore O hidden splendour Thee
Who in Thy sacrament dost deign to be
We worship Thee beneath this earthly veil
And here Thy Presence we devoutly hail

Priest: Almighty God, we pray that Your Angel may take this
Sacrifice to Your Altar on High.
There to be offered by them, Who as the Eternal High priest,
forever offer themself as the Eternal Sacrifice

And as He has willed that the Heavenly Sacrifice shall be mirrored
here on earth, so that Your people may be united more closely to You,
We pray for Your servants, Who minister at this altar,
That by celebrating these Mysteries, of the Divine Body + and
Blood + They may be filled + with Your Mighty Power and Blessing

Minor Elevation

Priest: By + Him, with + Him and in + Him,
In the unity of the Holy Spirit,
All Glory and Honour is Yours Almighty God
Forever and ever

Congregation: Amen

Fraction

Priest: O Son of God, You show Yourself this day upon
countless altars,
Yet, truly remain One and Indivisible, In token of Your Great
Sacrifice, we break (breaking of the Hosts) this Your Body

And in token of Your triumph over + death, and the Oneness of
Your + Spirit and body, and Your Glorious + Resurrection, we unite
this Your Body, with this Your Blood (unite). Praying that by this
action ordained from old, they may be for us, and for all the world,
a Channel of Grace and of Life Eternal.

Congregation: Amen

Communion rite

(Priest gives out communion)

Priest:
The Body of Christ + and the Bread of Angels,
The Blood of Christ + and the Grail of Eternal Life

Ablutions / meditation

Post communion prayer

Priest: I have eaten Your Sacred Body, no darkness will take me,
I have looked upon it, now my eyes see Your Wonders,
I have not been a stranger to Your Mysteries,
I am never separated from You ☦

Conclusion

Priest: The Blessings of God the Creator, the Redeemer + and
the transforming Spirit

Congregation: Amen

Priest: Ite Missa est

Congregation: Deo Gratias

The Holy Mass of Christ & Magdalena

A.S.A. APOSTOLIC SUCCESSION OF ARIMATHEA

Opening: stillness, invocation, procession and chant to the altar

(Priest enters and stands before the altar. A moment of silence…)

Invocation

Christ: This is the Day God has made

Congregation: Let us rejoice and be glad

Magdalena: The Light has entered the First Day

Christ: I will go up to the Altar of God

Congregation: Even unto the God of my joy and gladness

Christ: Send forth Thy Light and Thy Truth, that they may lead me, and bring me unto Thy Holy Hill and to Thy Dwelling Place

Magdalena: Know that your body is a Temple of the Holy Spirit, living within you, the Breath you have received at birth

Congregation: And I will go up to the Altar of God, even unto the God of my joy and Gladness

Christ & Magdalena: In the Name of God, the Creator, the ✠ Redeemer and the Transforming Spirit

Congregation: Amen

(Priest performs Asperges)
Priest: "Only through water and fire shall you enter the Kingdom of Heaven"

Magdalena: Fire is above water and the sky is above earth.
All of these are above and below and all are joined in the Mother's
Womb which is the Primordial Space from which they all arise

Congregation: All Encompassing One, Who ceaselessly creates
and sustains the fabric of the Universe, send forth Your Holy and
Beloved Angels, to guard, encourage, protect and teach all who dwell
within this place.
In Your strength O God, do we command all adverse powers,
to wither into nothingness; that they shall not abide, and that our
temples ☩ within, and our temples ☩ without, may emerge as strong,
pure vessels, to contain the Eternal Mystery, as it unfolds on earth

Congregation: Amen

Lighting of the Four Candles

(Christ speaks and Magdalena light the candles)

Christ: I will kindle my fire this Day / night
In the Presence of the four Archangels of Heaven
In the Presence of Raphael, regent of the Air
In Presence of Michael, regent of the Fire
In Presence of Gabriel, regent of the Waters
In Presence of Uriel, regent of the Earth

Magdalena: Without malice, without jealousy,
Without envy, without fear,
Without terror of anyone under the sun

Congregation: God, Kindle Thou in my heart within,
A flame of love to my neighbour,
To my foe, to my friend, to my kindred and all,
To the brave, to the knave, to the thrall,
The Blessings of Heaven be upon us,
From the lowliest creature that liveth,
To the Name that is highest of all,
Amen

Purification & First censing

Christ: Purify this place O God, and make of us One Body,
Growing into the Fullness of Christ - Magdalena
A Temple of Living Stones, through which Infinite Life may flow,
Let the Angels and Archangels join us in this Work of transforming
the earth

(Magdalena holds and presents the skull)
Magdalena: This world is a cemetery. It is filled with corpses, for
this reason Christ set the world on fire so that the dead might awaken
and spirits might be set free.
And now the fire burns and we tend it so that it might burn brightly,
dancing within the fire, with the Spirit of God. If you seek the
Anointed you seek the fire, and when you are utterly burnt away,
you will rejoice in the True Light

Congregation: Amen

Addressing penitential rite

Christ: My companions, beloved ones, to prepare ourselves to receive
and celebrate the Sacred Mysteries, let us make our confession before
God and the Mother for she gives to her children all they desire

All: Create in me a clean heart. O forgiving Love,
And renew a right Spirit within me,
Here is my body, I cast it down before you,
Heal its imperfections with your perfection and make me whole.
Here is my mind, I spread it out before you,
Forgive my foolishness and ignorance with Your bright wisdom.
Here is my heart, it is Yours alone,
Forgive its restless wanderings from You.
Here is my life, I offer it unto You,
Do with me as You will, forgive me,
Together with yourself, restore unto me, the Joy of Your Salvation,
That I may awake in Your likeness and be satisfied,
Through Christ, the Indwelling Light,
Amen

Absolution

Christ: The Mercy and Grace of God be upon you ✠ will forgive
yourself and all others and bring us to Eternal Light

Magdalena: Do not be concerned with the darkness in the world but
banish the darkness that is in you, for it will bind you and destroy
you if you do not cast it out

Congregation: Amen

KYRIE

Congregation:
KYRIE ELEISON, KYRIE ELEISON. KYRIE ELEISON
CHRISTE ELEISON, CHRISTE ELEISON, CHRISTE ELEISON
KYRIE ELEISON, KYRIE ELEISON, KYRIE ELEISON

Gloria

Christ: Glory be to God, the Inmost and Most Highest

Congregation: And peace to its people on earth. Almighty God our
Father - Mother, we worship You, we give You thanks, we praise
You for Your Glory,
Christ, all redeeming One, Son of the Great Light, Help and Heal us all
You are seated at the right hand of the Father, receive our prayer,
For You are the Chief among the Holy Ones, You are the Anointed,
The Beloved Child, at Your left resides the Magdalena, who with
the Holy Spirit, are One in the ✠ Glory of God

Congregation: Amen

Collect

Magdalena: The Light be with you

Congregation: And also with you

Christ: Let us pray

All:
O God the Giver of all gifts,
We praise You, the Source of all we have and are.
You shelter us beneath the shadow of Your Wings,
And search into the depths of our hearts,
Your Light is strong, your Love is here,
Remove the blindness that cannot know You, and relieve the fear
that would hide us from Your Sight,
Touched by Your Hand, our world is Holy,
Open our eyes to see Your hand at work in the Splendor of Creation,
and the beauty of human life,
Draw us beyond the limits, which this world imposes,
To the Life where Your Spirit makes all life complete,
We ask this through Your Son the Christ, your Child,
Who lives and reigns with You, conjoined with the Magdalena
and the Holy Spirit, One God, forever and ever. Amen

Liturgy of the word

Magdalena: There are seven Heavens, seven earths and seven hells
and there are worlds within worlds and realms within realms.
All shall pass away but the Supernal abode shall abide Eternal.
There is no end to Gods Word or Wisdom
Then Peter said to Yahushua: Since you have explained everything
to us, tell us one more thing. What is the sin of this world?
Yahushua replied: Sin as such does not exist. You only bring it into
manifestation when you act in ways that are adulterous in nature.
It is for this very reason that the Good has come among you pursuing
its own essence within nature in order to reunite everything to its
origin.... this is also the reason for sickness and death, because
you embrace what deceives you.

Consider these matters, then, with your spiritual intellect....
attachment to matter gives birth to passion without an image of itself
because it is drawn from that which is contrary to its higher nature.
The result is that confusion and disturbance resonates throughout
one's whole being. It is for this reason that I told you to find
contentment at the level of the heart, and if you are discouraged,
take heart in the presence of the image of your true nature.
Those with ears, let them hear.

Gradual

Christ: Whoever loves Wisdom, loves life; and they that seek her
early, shall be filled with joy. Teach us, O God, the Path to Your
Mystery, and I shall keep it unto the end. Give me understanding
and I shall keep Your Law; I shall keep it with whole my heart,
For the path of the Just is as the Shining Light, shining more
and more unto that Perfect Day

Invocation Christ: Cleanse my heart and my lips O Most High,
Who by the hand of your Angel-Seraph, did cleanse the lips of your
Prophets with that of a burning coal from Your Altar. And in Your
loving - kindness, purify me, that I may proclaim the Holy Gospel

May the Divine be in my ✜ heart and on my ✜ lips, that through my
heart the Love of God may shine forth and my mouth may manifest
Its Power

Congregation: Amen

Christ: The second reading is from the Corpus Hermeticum
called "Apprehension"

If then you do not make yourself equal unto God, you cannot
apprehend God; For like calls to like.
Leap clear of all that is corporeal, and make yourself grow to a like
expanse, with that greatness which is beyond all measure;
Rise above all time and become eternal, then you will
apprehend God.

Think that for you nothing is impossible, deem that you too are
immortal, and that you are able to grasp all things in your thought,

To know every craft and every science; find yourself home in the
haunts of every living creature; make yourself higher then all heights
and lower then all depths; bring together in yourself all opposites
of quality: heat and cold, dryness and fluidity; think that you are
everywhere at once, on land, at sea, in heaven; think that you are
not yet begotten, that you are in the womb, that you are young,
that you are old, that you have died, that you are in the world beyond
the grave; grasp in your thoughts all this at once; all times and places,
all substances and qualities and magnitudes together. Then you can
apprehend God.

For it is the height of evil not to know God; but to be capable
of knowing God, and to wish to and hope to know Him,
Is the road which leads straight to the Good"

Christ: This is the Word and Work of the Light

Congregation: Thanks be to the Eternal and Beloved One

Magdalena: The Light be with you

Congregation: And also with you

Meditation

Credo

All:
I Believe in God the Divine Mystery, beyond all definition
and all rational understanding, the Heart of all that has ever existed,
that exists now and ever will exist,

I Believe in Yahushua, Messenger of God's Word, Bringer
of Gods Healing, Heart of Gods Compassion, Bright Star
in the Firmament, of Gods Prophets, Mystics and Saints,

I Believe in the Holy Spirit, the Life of God that is our innermost Life,
The Breath of God moving in our Being, the Depth of God Living
in each of us,
A new-born I am, coming from the Womb of the Divine Mother
where every day I am taught by the ways of the Magdalena,

I Believe that I am called to be Yahushua's Twin, allowing myself
to be a vehicle of God's Love, a source of Gods Wisdom and Truth,
and an instrument of Gods Peace in the World,

I Believe that Gods Reign is here and now, stretched out all around
us for those with eyes to see it, hearts to receive it and hands to
make it happen,

I Believe in the community of God seekers, in all religions,
the prophets, mystics and saints, and those just beginning their
Spiritual Journey,

I Believe in a future on this earth, when all will be God-centred
and God conscious; when we will learn to live in Peace and Love,
in the fellowship of brothers and sisters,

I Believe in the power of endless compassion and forgiveness
brought about by Mary Magdalena, who is the Light in the world,
bringer of beauty and the greater understanding of Life,

I Believe that in death life is changed, not taken away and that
we will always go, from step to step in Gods Life, Gods Love
and Gods Glory for All Eternity. Amen - Amen - Amen

Sign of Peace

Christ: My companions, we have washed and burned away our
ignorance and we have been forgiven; Christ and Magdalena
the Compassionate King and Queen, bind us with a bond of Love that
cannot be broken. Therefore in the Name of the Logos ever present
ever saying:

"Peace I leave with you, my Peace I give unto you, not as the world gives do I give it unto you"

Christ and Magdalena: The Peace of Christ be with you always

All: And also with you

Presentation of the Gifts

(Priest lifts Shroud from the Grail and Paten)

Priest: Leave the mortal and the temporal to the realm of the world, for they are as dust and ash, while I am Immortal and Eternal amongst you. Behold Me as I Am and behold your own face within Me (presentation Shroud)

(Christ raises paten)

Christ: Most Holy One, accept that of which by the nature of this planet we are composed, and in our great gratitude, we offer this Bread unto You, as we likewise offer ourselves,

Congregation: On this paten Oh Christ, with this Bread, we place all the creative actions of the peoples of the earth; their aspirations, their joy, their achievements and their work,

Christ: Blessed are You, God of all creation. Through Your Goodness we have this Bread to offer, which earth has given and human hands have made.
It will become for us, our ✟ Bread of Life

All: Blessed be God forever

(Magdalena and Christ fill the cup)

Magdalena and Christ: "As your Spirit would move the heart of every being…now we move water within this wine, and they shall move as one"

Magdalena: We adore you O God, and offer unto You this Water
and Wine, as we offer that which gives us life. From You have we
come and unto You shall we return

Congregation: Into our Chalice with this Wine, we pour the sorrows,
the pain and the suffering of all your creation. Into this offering of
the world, we would gather, those closest to us, those whose lives
are bound up with our own

Magdalena: Blessed are You God of all creation, through Your
Goodness we have this Wine to offer; fruit of the vine and work
of human hands
It will become for us our ☦ Spiritual Drink

All: Blessed be God forever

Sign of Bondage

All: With these we unite those more distant and less familiar to us,
The great multitude of humanity, scattered over every part
of the globe,
In deepest sympathy and understanding, we unite ourselves,
With the ceaseless pilgrimage of humanity; past, present and future,
With all its joys and sorrows, its hopes and fears,
That we may be one with it All. We would draw into this offering
every form of Life: animals, trees, flowers and fruits, rocks and fire,
wind and water, and the very fabric of the earth itself,
We offer ourselves, all that we have and all that we are,
Let all existence be now placed on our altar, that we may raise
it up to Thee

Congregation: Amen

Second Censing

(Christ performs censing of the offerings, Shroud and the congregation)
Magdalena: How can I come to know the Light? And Mary said:
become empty like a Cup and let Spirit and the Presence of Christ
be poured into you

(Christ lifts paten and chalice)

Christ: Receive O Source of Life, this Your manifold Creation, in all its Light and all its Darkness

All: Amen

Prayer over the gifts

Christ: Most Holy One, by these Holy Gifts we offer, make ✢ Holy those who gather in Your Name. May we who share this sacrament, experience the life and power it promises and enter Your Presence. *Congregation:* Amen

Magdalena: Unless you know the Kingdom in you, you will not see it outside of you, and unless the Anointed indwells you, you will not find the Anointed in the world

Sursum Corda

Christ: The Light be with you
All: And also with you

Magdalena: Lift up your hearts
All: We lift them up to the most High

Christ: Let us give thanks to God
All: It is right to give thanks and praise

Preface

Magdalena: O Holy One of Blessing, God of all being, we do well always and everywhere to give you thanks
You have no need of our praise, yet our desire to thank you is itself your gift. Our prayer of thanksgiving adds nothing to Your Greatness, but makes us to grow in Your Grace
You give us Your Holy Spirit, the Comforter, to help us always with Her Power, so that with loving trust, we may turn to You in all our troubles and give You thanks in all our joys

Christ: Source of Life and Goodness, you have created all things,
To fill Your creatures with every Blessing, and lead all to the joyful
vision of Your Light. Countless Hosts of Angels, stand before You,
to do Your Will. They look upon You, and praise you night and day.
United with them, with Angels and Archangels, with Thrones,
Dominations, Princedoms, Virtues and Powers, with Cherubim,
Seraphim and Ashim, and in the Name of every creature under
Heaven, we too praise Your Glory as we say:

Sanctus

All: Holy! Holy! Holy! God of power and might
Heaven and earth are full of Your Glory
Hosanna in the Highest
Blessed are those who come in the Name of the Holy One
Hosanna in the Highest

Canon of the Mass

Christ: God You are Holy indeed, the Fountain of all Holiness,
As one family we gather around Your Table,
Here is the sacrifice of Christ and Magdalena offered in mystery

Here is prepared the Table of Light, at which Your children,
Are nourished by the Body of Christ,
Here Your people drink from the Living Spirit,
The stream of Living Water, that flows from the Stone of Christ.
Loving Creator, we bring You all these gifts of Bread ✠ and Wine ✠
And ourselves as a living sacrifice

Let Your Spirit descend upon these gifts, to make them Holy;
Sanctify them, that they may become-
The Body ✠ and Blood ✠ of Christ,
Who has willed us to make this Eucharist

Consecration

Christ: The day before He suffered He took Bread into His
Sacred Hands,
And with His Eyes lifted up to Heaven, He gave You thanks
and praise.
He broke and ✠ blessed the Bread, giving it unto His disciples, saying:

"Take and eat this all of you, for:
This is My Body"

When supper was ended, He took this Cup into His Sacred Hands,
Again He gave You thanks and praise. He blessed ✠ the Cup,
and gave it unto His disciples saying:

"Take and drink this all of you, for:
This is the Cup of My Blood"

Christ and Magdalena whisper: Whenever you do these things
I AM is present among you.

Magdalena: There is light and fire in your Living Breath. If you
cleave to the Risen Saviour and breathe as the Saviour breathes you
will find it. Thereafter your whole body will be filled with fire and
Light, and be transformed into the image of the Holy Living One
(all are given a light / candle from the altar)

Affirmation

All: Thee we adore O hidden splendour Thee
Who in Thy sacrament dost deign to be
We worship Thee beneath this earthly veil
And here Thy Presence we devoutly hail

Christ: Father, we celebrate the Mystery of Christ, we Your people
and Your ministers, recall His incarnation and Passion,
His triumphant resurrection from the dead and His ascension into
Your Glory

And from the many Gifts You have given us, we offer to You,
God of Glory and Majesty, this Holy and Perfect Sacrifice:
The Bread ✟ of Life and the Cup of ✟ Eternal Salvation

Magdalena: Look with favour on these offerings and accept them
as once you accepted the Gifts of Abraham and Sarah, our parents
in faith, the anointing of Mary Magdalena at the feet of Christ,
and the Wine and Bread offered by Your Priest, Melchizedek

Christ: Almighty God, we pray that Your Angel may take this
Sacrifice to Your Altar on High. There to be offered by Him, Who as
the Eternal High Priest, forever offers himself as the Eternal Sacrifice
And as He has willed that the Heavenly sacrifice shall be mirrored
here on earth, so that Your people may be united more closely to You,
We pray for Your servants, who minister at this Altar,
That by celebrating these Mysteries, of the Divine Body ✟
and Blood ✟
They may be filled ✟ with Your Mighty Power and Blessing

Congregation: Amen

Magdalena: Loving God, we call You Father, but you are
the Fountain of Motherhood, male and female You created us,
in Your own image and likeness.
May all people come to know, that in You, there is no male or female,
No distinction between race, class or colour,
For we are all one within You

All: Through Christ, You give us all these gifts
You fill them with Life and Goodness
You Bless them and make them Holy

Minor Elevation

Christ: By ✟ Him, with ✟ Him, and in ✟ Him,
In the Unity of the Holy Spirit,
All Glory and Honour is Yours Almighty God
Forever and Ever

Congregation: Amen

Magdalena: Here you are, and here I Am, and here is the Eternal Light

Christ's Prayer

All: Oh Thou, from Whom the Breath of Life comes,
Who fills all Realms of Sound, Light and Vibration,
May Your Light be known in my utmost Holiest of Being
Your Heavenly Domain approaches, let Your Will come true,
on earth as it is in Heaven,

Give us Wisdom for our daily need and detach the fetters of our
faults that bind us, like we let go the guilt of others
And let us not be lost in worldly things, but let us be free from what
keeps us from our true purpose,
From You comes the all-working Will, the Lively Strength to act,
the Song that Beautifies all, and renews itself from age to age
Sealed in Love, Faith and Truth. Amen, Amen, Amen

Fraction

Christ: O Son of God, You show Yourself this day upon countless altars,
Yet, truly remain One and Indivisible, in token of Your great
Sacrifice, we break (Ø) this, Your Body. And in token of Your
Triumph over ✙ death, and the oneness of Your ✙ Spirit and body,
and Your Glorious Resurrection, we unite this Your Body, with this
Your Blood

Magdalena: Praying that by this Action, ordained from old, they may
be for us, and for all the world, a channel of Grace and of Life Eternal

Congregation: Amen

Agnus Dei

Christ: Lamb of God, slain from the Foundation of the world

Congregation: Help and Heal us all

Christ: Lamb of God, slain from the Foundation of the world

Congregation: Help and Heal us all

Christ: Lamb of God, slain from the Foundation of the world

Congregation: Grant us Peace

Magdalena: This is the Lamb of God slain from the Foundation of
the world, happy are those who take place at His Supper

Magdalena: Christ our Passover is sacrificed for us, therefore let us
keep the feast. As You gave Your Body and Blood, so too I offer
myself wholly unto You; My Body and my Blood, to transform as
You Will, that Your Mystery is completed within me ✠

Communion

(Christ gives out communion)

The Body of Christ ✠ and the Bread of Angels,
The Blood of Christ ✠ and the Grail of Eternal Life

Post communion prayer

Magdalena: I have eaten Your sacred Body, no darkness will take me
I have looked upon it, now my eyes see Your Wonders
I have not been a stranger to Your Mysteries
I am never separated from You ✠

Conclusion

Christ: let us pray

All: Under the veil of earthly things, now have we communion with
the Light of Christ. With open face we do see Him, and being made
anew, like unto His own Glorious Body, may we abide in Your
Presence always O God,
And serve You night and day - Amen

Magdalena: Behold your own face in me and hear …my beloved
and loyal ones, you who in this mortal life, have become spiritual
creatures and who sought me so diligently… that I cannot hide
myself from your eyes

Christ: The Mystery is complete and the rite is ended and the Blessed
Archangels depart in Joy and Peace

All: We give thanks to all the Holy Angels of Heaven and to God
Who send them

Magdalena: The Blessing of God the Creator, the Redeemer ✚ and
the Transforming Spirit - Amen

Christ: Ite Missa est

All: Deo Gratias

Holy Mass of Archangel Raphael (Healing Mass)

A.S.A. APOSTOLIC SUCCESSION OF ARIMATHEA

Offered with the intention of Healing for another. Entry Clergy with Chalice, Staff and chanting YHVH

Priest: Oh you Angels of the Most Holy One, Bless the Christ and all the Companions of The Way, praise them and Magnify them forever

All: To them all Angels sing aloud, the Heavens and all the Powers therein

Priest: To them Cherubim and Seraphim continually cry

All: Holy, Holy, Holy, Thou the Eternal Hosts

Priest: Oh praise the Holy One, you Angels of Ministry, you Strong Ones who fulfil Christ's Commands and hear its Voice

All: Oh praise the One, all Celestial Hosts, you servants that perform the primordial Will

Collects

Priest: Let us pray

Eternal God, with all our hearts we praise You for the Celestial Glory of Your ministering Spirits, especially Holy Archangel Raphael and all Your Healing Angels. In Your Love and Light, Oh Christ of the Heavenly Hosts, You give us the assistance of these Your Radiant Servants and so we thank You for their Wonderful Wisdom, their Supreme Strength and their abiding Beauty through Christ, the King of Angels

All: Amen

Aspergil

(Priest performs Aspergil - three times priest, three times the altar
and three times the congregation)

Priest: All Encompassing One, Who ceaselessly Creates and Sustains
the fabric of the Universe, send forth Your Holy and Beloved Angels,
To guard, encourage, protect and teach all who dwell within
this place.
In Your Strength O God, do we command all adverse powers,
to wither into nothingness; that they shall not abide,
And that our temples + within, and our temples + without,
May emerge as strong, pure vessels,
To contain the Eternal Mystery, as it unfolds on earth

All: Amen

Lighting of the Four candles

Priest: I will kindle my fire this day,
In the Presence of the Four Archangels of Heaven,
In the Presence of Raphael, regent of the Air,
In Presence of Michael, regent of the Fire
In Presence of Gabriel, regent of the Waters
In Presence of Uriel, regent of the Earth,

Without malice, without jealousy,
Without envy, without fear,
Without terror of anyone under the sun

All: God, Kindle Thou in my heart within,
A flame of love to my neighbour,
To my foe, to my friend, to my kindred and all,
To the brave, to the knave, to the thrall,
The Blessings of Heaven be upon us,
From the lowliest creature that liveth,
To the Name that is Highest of all,
Amen

First censing: (invocation of the Angel of Christ)

Priest: Purify this place O God, and make of us One Body,
Growing into the Fullness of Christ,
A Temple of Living Stones, through which Infinite Life may flow,
Let the Angels and Archangels join us in this Work of transforming
the Earth

Priest: Oh God, You are the Strength of all those who put their trust
in You. Without You nothing is strong, nothing is pure and Holy.
We commend to Your Infinite Loving-kindness,
Your daughter(s) / son(s), N.... who is / are in sickness and suffering,
so that as far as is expedient for them, they may receive full health
and thus serve You, through Christ the Great Physician

All: Amen

Epistle - This reading is from the Book of Tobit

And the Angel said to them. "Bless the Holy One, praise and magnify
God for the things God has done for you in the sight of all that
lives.... Those that exercise righteousness shall be filled with Life, but
they that sin are enemies to their own life. God send me to heal you
and your daughter, for I am Raphael, One of the Seven Holy Angels
who present the prayers of the righteous and go in and out before the
Glory of the Holy One".
Being fearful they fell upon their faces, but the Angel said, "Fear not,
it shall be well with you. Not by my favour, but by the Will of the
Holy One I came, therefore praise and thank the Holy One forever,
for I go up to the One who has sent me"
Then they spoke of the wonderful and great Works of God, saying:
"Blessed are You Oh God and blessed is Your Name forever and
blessed are all Your Holy Angels"

Priest: This is the Word of God

All: Thanks and love be to God. Amen

Gospel

Priest: God be with you

All: And also with you

Priest: A reading from the Holy Gospel according to John

Glory + be to + You, Oh + Christ

In Jerusalem by the sheep market was a pool named in Hebrew
'Bethesda' and around it were five porches. In these porches great
numbers of very sick people would gather, waiting for the surface
of the pool's waters to become agitated. This was because at certain
times, a healing Angel would descend into the pool causing
the waters to move. The person who first entered the pool, while
the waters moved, was healed of their disease. A certain man was
there who had been crippled for thirty-eight years. Seeing him,
Yahushua knew that he had been prostrate for a long time and
Yahushua asked him: "Do you want to be made whole"?
The sick man answered: "Master, I have no one to help me into
the healing pool when the waters are moving.... Before I can get there
others enter before me".
Yahushua replied: "Rise and take up your bed and walk"!
Immediately, the man was healed and so he could take up his bed
and walk away.

Priest: This is the Gospel of the Anointed

All: Praise be to you Oh Christ

Presentation of the Gift

(Before offering up the wafer and praying "Most Holy One...."
clearly and intently visualize the face of the person for whom
the Mass is offered, being at-one with the wafer. See and sense
the person being one with the bread so that the atoms of the bread are
mentally impregnated with their image and therefore physically
linked with them. Then during the consecration, when the wafer

is transmuted into the Sacred Host, the person will be united with
the deathless Body of Christ)

Priest: Remember that you are sick because you are deprived of
The One who is your healing. Open yourself unto Christ: EMPATHA!

(Priest raises Paten)

Priest: Most Holy One, accept that of which by the nature of this
planet we are composed, and in our great gratitude, we offer this
Bread unto You, as we likewise offer ourselves
Blessed are You, God of all creation. Through Your Goodness we
have this Bread to offer, which earth has given and human hands
have made. It will become for us, our + Bread of Life.

All: Blessed be God forever

(Priest fills the Cup)

Priest: As your Spirit would move the heart of every being,
Now we move water within this wine, and they shall move as one

Priest: We adore you O God, and offer unto You this Water and
Wine, as we offer that which gives us Life. From You have we come
and unto You shall we return
Blessed are You God of all creation, through Your Goodness we
have this wine to offer, fruit of the vine and work of human hands.
It will become for us our + Spiritual drink

All: Blessed be God forever

Second Censing

Prayer after the second censing

Priest: O most Holy One, we ask You to receive these Gifts, which
we offer for the Healing of your daughter / son, N....
All: Amen

Healing Rite

Priest: All who wish to be healed in this Sacrament in the Presence
of Christ and by the aid and support of Archangel Raphael, let them
bow before the altar (all who wish come forward and kneel before
the altar and all receive unction on heart, throat, third eye and top
of the head. People stand and wait for communion)

Prayer before communion

Priest: I will take up the Bread of Heaven and call upon the Name
of God. May the Body of Christ bring Healing to N.... Child(ren)
of God.

All: Amen

Priest: I will take up the Chalice of Salvation and call upon
the Name of God. May the Blood of Christ bring Healing to
N.... Child(ren) of God.

All: Amen

Fraction

Priest: O Son of God, You show Yourself this day upon countless altars,
Yet, truly remain One and indivisible,
In token of Your great Sacrifice, we break (breaking of the Host) this,
Your Body…

And in token of Your Triumph over ✠ death, and the oneness
of Your ✠ Spirit and Body, and Your Glorious ✠ Resurrection,
we unite this Your Body, with this Your Blood (unite).... Praying that
by this action ordained from old, they may be for us, and for all
the world, a channel of Grace and of Life Eternal. Amen

Communion

After Communion prayer

May Christ the Anointed of God, mediate Healing unto N.... and
enfold her / him in the Light Divine

All: Amen

Concluding Rite

Priest: Let us pray O Holy One; may these Sacred Mysteries bring
wholeness to your Child(ren) (N....). May Raphael and the Healing
Angels minister her / him according to Your Will, we ask this through
Christ, Your Light within us

All: Amen

Ash-Wednesday
(if the healing service is on Ash-Wednesday, the following rite
is included)

Priest: Now that the Light of Christ has been born and shines over
the earth, the darkness cannot hide any longer + and the Solar Logos
approaches with the Fire and Light of Love and our sins and
misdeeds will be incinerated.
Confess before Christ and the Holy One the wrong paths that
you have chosen so that they are turned + and made into pathways
of Gold....
Let the Sun shine at night, your inner eye be opened so no ignorance
shall blind you any longer + and the burned wrongdoings of the past
leave you like ash and dust in the wind

Priest: Remember the Path you have chosen, follow the Way
of Christ like Joseph of Arimathea and the other disciples.
Your inner and outer ways are purified in this moment of atonement
with Christ and the One-Who-is Openness + Receive the Cross of
Ash and see from this day forward with the Eye of Non-Duality,
the Eye of Christ (Priest makes the cross of ash on all present)

All: So we will remember and go forth on the Way of Christ

Priest: In the Name of the Holy One, the Name of Christ and
the Followers of the Way, that you may walk on that straight
and narrow Path of Truth

All: Amen

Holy Mass of Camelot
(Round Table)

A.S.A. APOSTOLIC SUCCESSION OF ARIMATHEA

All enter and the invocation of the Son of Light is recited

Priest: In the Name of the Son of Light, the Son of Maria,
Foster-son of Brighd in Avalon, Keystone of the Arch of Heaven,
Who joins as One, the forks upholding the sky,
His the right hand, His the left hand, His the rainbow letters,
All in rich fermented milk, we will go in his name,
In all shape of shapes, in all colors of colors,
Unto the Path to Peace.
It is the Son of Light, the Son of Maria, saying;
Speak in my Name and Peace shall be given unto you,
Enter in my Name and you shall in no wise be cast out,
Do you see us here O Son of Light?
Says the Son of Light:
I see ✠

Priest: This is the Day of the Son of Light

All: Let us gather at the Round Table

Priest: I will go to that place of meeting at the Great Hall of Camelot

All: At that sacred centre where all directions meet

Priest: Send forth Your Light and your Truth, that they may lead me,
bring me to the Holy Isle of Avalon, where lies Your dwelling place

All: And we will go up to the Kingdom of Camelot, the Kingdom
of Heaven

Priest: In the Name of Son of Light, the Creator, the ✠ Redeemer
and the Transforming Spirit

All: Amen

(Priest purifies with Awen)

All: All Encompassing One, Who ceaselessly creates and sustains
the fabric of the Universe, send forth Your Holy and Beloved Angels,
To guard, encourage, protect and teach all who dwell within
this place
In Your strength O Son of Light, do we command all adverse powers,
to wither into nothingness, that they shall not abide, and that our ☥
temples within, and our temples ☥ without, may emerge as strong,
pure vessels, to contain the Eternal Mystery, as it unfolds on earth

All: Amen

Lighting of the Four Candles

Priest: We will kindle our fire this Day, in the Presence of the four
Archangels of Heaven;
In the Presence of Raphael, regent of the Air, and the city of Gorias
In Presence of Michael, regent of the Fire, and the city of Finias
In Presence of Gabriel, regent of the Waters, and the city of Murias
In Presence of Uriel, regent of the Earth, and the city of Falias

All: Without malice, without jealousy, without envy, without fear,
without terror of anyone under the sun

Purification with Incense

Priest: Purify this place O Son of Light, and make of us One Body,
Growing into the Fullness of your Image and Likeness,
May we heal from all that binds us, restore this world from all
that keeps us in darkness and ignorance and help us to restore
the Land and this earthly Kingdom

All: Create in us a clean heart and renew the Spirit of Chivalry within me
Here is my body, I cast it down before the Grail
Heal its imperfections with the Awen of Heaven
Here is my mind, may the Wisdom of Avalon brighten it

Here is my heart, open to the Old Ways of Merlin and Morgana
Here is my life, I offer it unto the Quest for the Holy Grail
Restore unto me, the joy of Your Healing, and the healing
of the Land and Kingdom
That we may rise into the Glory of your Being, Oh Son of Light,
Amen

Priest: The Mercy and Grace of the Son of Light be upon you ☥
will forgive you and bring us to Eternal Light

All: Amen

All:
Un Ydw i'
Un Ydw i'
Un Ydw i'

Priest: Glory be to the Son of Light, the Inmost and Most Highest

All: And Peace to its people on the earthly kingdom and Logres.
Most Holy One, Who has brought the Grail to mankind,
all redeeming and liberating Light, we know You are within us,
as the Source of Love and all Wisdom,
May we follow in your footsteps to the Summer Lands,
and bring the Grail Home. Amen

Collect

Priest: The Son of Light be with you

All: And also with you

Priest: Let us pray

All: O Holy One the Giver of our Souls, let us live in Nobility,
We praise You, provider of Love and the Laws of the Round Table,
You protect us when danger is upon us, and comfort us when
we despair. Our hearts belong to you, while we give ourselves
to your Life and Purpose,

To love for Love's sake is the power of the Son of Light,
Remove the blindness on our path, and give us strenght to face
our fears,
Touched by Your Sacred Hand and guided by Your Lamp,
our pathway is lit,
And we find the courage to continue our Quest and face
our opponents,
Let us overcome our own boundaries and walk out of our
self-constructed Labyrinth, to cross the Sword-Bridge and
be in Your Presence, Son of Light,
You, the Immanence of the Transcendent Life within All,
One Being, forever and ever
Amen

Liturgy of Camelot Readings

(The first reading is from Sir Lancelot's stories)
Once I rescued a Lady from a Tree who had climed in
the branches, but could not get down. I took off all of my armour to
go to her rescue. As I was within her reach, a black knight came from
the forest, standing at the foot of the tree, waiting to slay me as soon
as I came down. I was trapped in the tree and by both persons fooled.
I had only my courage and a branch to fight the knight in full armour.
I jumped down and fought with my heart, won the battle by inner
strength and not by the outer weapons and iron that I was wearing.
The true strength lies within. All else is an extension of our inner life.

Priest: This is the Word of Lancelot, the Greatest Knight that ever lived

All: Thanks be to Lancelot, Grace to the Son of Light

Gradual

Priest: Whoever loves Wisdom, loves life, and they that seek the Grail will
find it on the path of their own Destiny. Be on your way through hardship
and joy. Teach us, O Son of Light, the Path to Your Mystery, and we shall
stay on our Quest. Give me understanding about the Ways of Avalon and
we will keep Your Law, and shall keep it with our whole heart.

(The second reading is from the Lady of the Lake)
One day I walked along my lake and saw Merlin sitting at a tree.
I changed my face and seduced him. First through my beauty, then
by way of promising him power and thirdly by magic. He resisted me
in all ways, and so I locked him up in a cave as he did not resist my
willpower. I did not know that it was only Merlin's body in that
cave… his mind and power were far beyond this prison at the lake.
From that day on, I knew that consciousness cannot be bound by
magic or the bars of an iron cell.

Priest: This is the Wisdom of Nimue, Lady of the Lake

All: Blessings to Nimue and Grace to the Son Of Light

Sermon (meditation) & Credo

All: I Believe in Sarras, the Divine home of the Grail, where all came
from and all will return. The Source of all beings and all creatures.

I Believe in Avalon, the Higher worlds where Laws are made and
the Miraculous works of the Spirit come down into the world.

I Believe in Camelot, the Kingdom of Heaven which is established by
the effort and consciousness of all seekers: past, present and future.

I Believe that the Son of Light lives within me and in all beings and
creatures, is my true being and the higher self within all the worlds.

I Believe in the Sovereignty of King and Queen in the world of Spirit
on earth, where Life, Light, Love and Law abide.

I Believe in the community of the Grail and all seekers, all those on
my Quest; the ones that help me and those that oppose me, that are
far ahead of me or those just beginning their Spiritual Journey.

I Believe in a Kingdom of Love, Peace and Righteousness, that was
founded by the Priest-Kings of old, in the order of Melchizadek and
under the guidance of the Priestesses of Avalon.

I Believe in the Apostolic Succession of Arimathea and the authethic
Teachings of Christ, the pureness of the Logos throughout all the ages.

I Believe that there is honour in living and in dying, and that we are
immortal Spirits that travell from eternity to eternity, forever within
the embrace of the Son of Light.
Amen

Presentation of the Gifts

(Priest lifts Shroud from the Grail and Paten)
Priest: See the Face of the Son of Light within your own face

(Priest raises paten)
Priest: As we have died many times and have arisen from those
ashes, we present to you this bread that represents our body,
as we walked from the dead like the immortal master of Light,
so we present our body as the vessel of the Immortal Grail.

All: So mote it be, now and forever more

(Priest fills the cup)
Priest: As the Light poured forth from the Otherworld, into the
natural realm of beast and humankind, now the Awen streams from
the Sacred Well and Spring, into the Cup of ultimate Healing, Love
and Peace. The Red and White streams flowing together as one.

All: Into our Sacred Chalice with the Awen, we receive the liquid
Light of the Otherworld, with all its virtues and spiritual gifts, so that
we may transmit them to others and the world at large. Remember
that the sacred vessel does not provide the waters of Otherworld
to liers and cowards.

(Priest raises Grail and Shield)
Priest: From the Summer Lands comes the everlasting Bliss

All: So mote it be, now and forever more

Sign of Bondage

All: Within these Gifts we unite the Otherworld, Avalon and Camelot
with the enchanted world of Logres and all its beings and creatures.
We connect to all seekers within every tradition and support the
pilgrimage of those honest souls who search and work for something
greater than themselves. Overcoming our fears, sorrows and anger,
to restore the wounded land and all therein.

We would draw into this Grail all those who have gathered at
Camelot and work for our Humanity in service of Spirit and the
Highest Source of All. May we share this Mystery with each other,
so that we transform through the Cup and its Heavenly meal upon
this Table Round. We are gathered here, where no fools are aloud,
no oath-breakers are accepted and where all companions await
the Miraculous Life to come.

Orate Fratres

Priest: Pray my companions, that our sacrifice may be acceptable
before the Teachers of Camelot, the Guardians of the Grail and
the Son of Light

All: May this sacrifice be accepted by the Sacred Council of Avalon
so that we transform into Kings and Queens within the Kingdom
of Heaven

Prayer over the gifts

Priest: Son of Light, draw closer and come amongst us, so that these
gifts may truly be sanctified and made Holy. We, who gather in
Your Name and in Your Power, Love and Wisdom (circled cross ☦)

Sursum Corda

Priest: The Son of Light be with you

All: And also with you

Priest: Lift up your hearts unto Avalon

All: We lift them up to the Island beyond the mists

Priest: Let us give thanks to the Son of Light

All: Our gratitude shines on our Quest

Preface

Priest: O Shining One of Blessing, Son of Light, Child of the Beloved,
We bring our gratitude and humbleness, for our Quest began with
the drawing of the Sword from Stone and the Oath of Chivalry.
You comfort us on our Quest, supporting us in time of need and
protect us when we are defenseless. You feed us when we are
starving and encourage us when we are devoid of the Spirit
of the Otherworld.
Son of the Great Light, you Who has come from the Womb
of the Mother who has brought us all into the World of Spirit,
You Who is the Cornerstone of all Life, the Waters flowing from
Heaven, the Wisdom inside the words of the Elders of Avalon.
You are the Inner Teacher of my Council, the life of this world
without end,
You, Who has called us on our Quest, for our souls to come home
and gather with You at the Round Table. Here we guide others,
so they too may follow in our example when seekers hear the call
from the Otherworld.

Canon of the Mass

All: Son of Light, You are the Sacred Child within the Grail indeed,
the Light within the Well, the blood, sweat and tears of our life
and journey
As one family we gather around Your Table, together with your
Disciples, the Companions, Joseph of Arimathea and all those who
followed You

Priest: We are nourished by Your Body and Your Awen, the two
streams joining together, here we drink from that Living Spirit,
the Stream of Living Water, that flows from Your Hands. Loving One
of Light, we bring You all these gifts of our Body ✠ and Awen ✠
and ourselves as a living sacrifice

All: Let us be transformed and become Grail-Bearers in this world,
in Camelot, the Place where Souls meet, and Logres, the world
of ignorance.

Consecration

Priest: The day the Grail descended for the first time upon the Round
Table, and the Son of Light revealed itself unto us,
We received His Gifts of food and wine to nourish our souls,
our minds, hearts and body. The Gift of His Body was divided ✠
for the many, yet remained One and Spiritually whole.
From the Cup held in His Sacred Hands, came the streams of Red
and White ✠, the rivers of Spirit which nourish and transform our
earthly body into a vessel for the ways of Avalon.

All: From that day on, the companions of the Round Table vowed to
go on a Quest for the Grail and find You again, unveiled, so we may
surrender unto Your Grace and enter Your Presence.

Affirmation

All: Into Thine Arms we surrender, we yield our souls, as we
followed our Coat of Arms to come in Your midst, to become Bearers
of Secrets, an embodiment of Grace, and a saviour unto others.

Priest: We celebrate the Mystery of the Grail, we your children and
companions, having overcome the Wasteland, nurtured our soul-
wound and followed the Old Ways of King and Queen and
the Wisdom of Avalon. Behold the Round Table or Table of Stars
with its twelve constellations and the twelve tribes that form the
intelligences of this Mighty Company. Our division from the Grail
is our greatest suffering. Our union with the Grail is our greatest
healing and fulfillment.

All: Let us witness the sacred procession with the Grail in the hands
of the White Maiden, and ask the question of ultimate concern.
What do you need to be restored, and what does the world need to
be healed?

Priest: This is the Bread ✠ of Life and the Cup of ✠ Eternal Grace

All: We call upon the Nine Priestesses, Morgana of Avalon and its
High Priest Merlin. The Island of Holy Apples is open to us,
the Home of the Grail, Sarras, beckons us as we gather at this Table
of The Son of Light, in the Great Hall of Camelot.

Minor Elevation

Priest: By the ✠ Son, ✠ of, ✠ Light,
The Company of Avalon, the Otherworld and all its inhabitants,
all honour and light returns to you.

Communion rite

Priest: Behold My Beloved,
I have shown you the power of Silence, how thoroughly it heals and
how pleasing it is unto God.
Therefore I have written to you, to show yourselves, and be strong in
this work that you have undertaken,
So that you may know that it is, by Silence that the Saints grow,
By Silence that the Power of God dwells in them,
And through Silence that the Mysteries of God, are made known unto
them in the Body (fraction) that returns to its Grail (✠)

Communion

Priest: And Melchizedek King of Salem, brought forth Bread and
Wine, and he was Priest of the Most High God. And like unto Joseph
of Arimathea he gave the Blessing of Heaven so he might live.'
He Blessed Him / Her and said:
Blessed be (your name) of the Most High God, creator
of Heaven and Earth.

Meditation post Communio

All: We have eaten Your Sacred Body, and drank from Your Spirit
no darkness will take me, we have seen and embraced You,
Your Wonders, Miracles and Loving Presence
We are no strangers to Your Mysteries, we are always with You
and are never separated from You ☥

Conclusion

All: Under the veil of Avalon, now have we communion with the Son
of Light. We have found the Grail Castle and its court and will rest
like the Grail King, being restored and healed. Let us return to
the world and offer our service, wisdom and strength to continue
the Work of Light.

Priest: Let us close the Great Hall of Camelot and return to the forest
of Logres, you and I being companions; brothers and sisters in
this Great Kingdom

Ritual of the Questions
of Bartholomew

To be celebrated on the Day of Annunciation (23 March) or Day of
Bartholomew (24 of August) Holy Mass starts as usual or this ritual is
integrated in the Communion rite. After the "all encompassing One...."
and the lighting of the candles, the Rite of Bartholomew starts.

Priest: Companions, brothers and sisters, we are here gathered to
celebrate the greatest of all temple rituals: the Rite of Annunciation.
This is not an act of magic or a human act only, for here we do not
work with created realities. Our work lies within the ways of the
mystic and The Way of Christ. We seek the Divine agencies and call
upon the Angels and Archangels and all the Company of Heaven.
Being mindful of these things that I tell you, beloved companions,
let me open the temple so that the Mysteries may be revealed.

All: Amen

Priest: In the Holy Name of El Elyon, the Great Name uttered by
the High-Priest Melchizedek.

All: Not in forgetfulness, nor in utter nakedness, but in trailing clouds
of Glory do we come from God Who is our Home.

Priest: When Christ wished to come upon the earth for mankind,
the Father summoned a mighty power in Heaven which is called
Michael and entrusted to the care thereof.

All: And the power came into the world and was called Mary,
and Christ was in Her womb for Seven months.

Priest: So did the Son of Light descend the Sevenfold Ladder
of Lights, the Great Ladder seen by Jacob while asleep.

(Priest lights the lamps or candles on the altar with the usual words, before the purification / incensing)

Priest: And He was among us; Christ, Son of Mary - the Grail and the Shekinah.

All: Amen

Meditation

Priest: Let us now go to that sacred place in our vision, called the Mary Chapel. Close your eyes and sink in meditation, going into that Holy Place of meeting where we are amongst the Company of Christ. Become aware of the disciples like Joseph of Arimathea, Thomas, Salome, Philip, Mary Magdala, Nicodemus, Lazarus and many others.... Mary the Mother of Yahushua sits before the Veil of the Temple. She proclaims:
"This is the Land of the Cherubim, and this is my original country"!
See how a disciple comes to the front and stands before Mary.
It is our brother Bartholomew. He asks Mary....

Questions of Bartholomew

Bartholomew: Mary, tell us of your work in the temple and your purpose therein

Mary: Ask me not concerning this mystery for if I should begin to tell you, fire shall issue from my mouth and consume the world

Bartholomew: we will not leave before some mystery has been revealed to us Mary

Mary: Very well then, come O disciples of Christ, gather around me. Twenty-two letters are uttered in this temple and chief of these being called the Mother Letters - Shin, Aleph and Mem.... Shema!

Bartholomew: So we all felt the air grow loud with voices of unseen spirits and a voice as clear as water which flowed out of Eden spoke to us

Mary: When I abode in the temple of God and received my food
from an Angel, on a certain day there appeared to me one in the
likeness of an Angel, but its face was incomprehensible and did not
carry a Cup and Bread as did the Angel which came to me a foretime
And straight away the Veil of the temple was rent and there was
a great earthquake and Mary fell upon the earth for she was not able
to endure the sight of the Angel. That Angel put its arms and mighty
wings around me and raised me up

Bartholomew: And Mary looked up into Heaven and there came
a cloud of dew and sprinkled her from head to feet and the mighty
Angel wiped her with its robe and said unto her

Priest: Hail thou that art highly favoured, the chosen vessel of Grace
inexhaustible … and the Angel smote its garment on the right hand
and there appeared Bread.... and sat it upon the altar of
the temple.... The Angel ate of it and then gave also unto me
And Mary beheld and saw the Bread and the Cup whole as they are.
Yet three years and I will send my word unto thee and thou shalt
conceive my Son. Through Him shall the whole of creation be saved.
Peace be unto you my beloved and my Peace shall be with
you continually
And when he had said so, the Angel vanished away from our eyes
and the temple was restored as it had been before.

Bartholomew: Is it by Bread and Wine that the gates are opened
between heaven and earth?

Mary: It is so, for know this my children, that not in forgetfulness nor
in utter nakedness, but in trailing clouds of glory do we come from
God Who is our Home. And so I have told you that the mystery lies
in a piece of grain and grape, brought together.

Bartholomew & Mary: Hear o children for God grants that on our
return home we shall take with us the bounty of our being. Even the
creatures of the earth and those who have wardship over them. And
the firstborn of this earth, the Shining Ones that they may light our
way and we in turn may light their welcome.

May the chariot ascend filled with laughter and love of the good earth
and the light of the starry heavens. Peace to all signs and shadows,
light in all ways of darkness and the living Son of Light reborn forever

(Eucharist continues with the censing or the rite of Communion may
follow now)

Administration of
the Holy Communion

A.S.A. APOSTOLIC SUCCESSION OF ARIMATHEA

Invocation

Priest: In the Name of God, the Creator ✠, the Redeemer and
the Transforming Spirit.
Congregation: Amen

Priest: My brothers and sisters, companions and fellow-travellers
of The Way, to prepare ourselves to receive the Sacred Mysteries,
let us make our confession before God

All: Create in me a clean heart O Forgiving Love,
And renew a right Spirit within me.
Here is my body, I cast it down before You,
Heal its imperfections with Your Perfection and make me whole.
Here is my mind, I spread it out before You,
Forgive my foolishness and ignorance with Your Bright Wisdom.
Here is my heart, it is Yours alone,
Forgive its restless wanderings from You.
Here is my life, I offer it unto You,
Do with me as You will, forgive me,
Together with Yourself, restore unto me, the joy of Your Salvation,
That I may awake in Your Likeness and be satisfied,
Through Christ, the Indwelling Light,
Amen

Absolution

Priest: The Mercy and Grace of God be upon you ✠ will liberate
us from all sins and bring us to Eternal Light

Priest: let us pray with confidence to the Father, the One Who
is Openness in the words that Christ taught us

All: Our Father Who art in Heaven, Hallowed be Thy Name,
Thy Kingdom come, Thy Will be done,
On earth as it is in Heaven,
Give us this day our daily bread and forgive us our trespasses,
As we forgive those who trespass against us,
And lead us not into temptation, but deliver us from evil,
For Thine is the Kingdom ✠ and the Power and the Glory,
Forever and ever. Amen

Opening of the Tabernacle

Priest: O God the Life of worlds in this wonderful sacrament of
the altar. You have given us a living memorial of your endless love
for humanity, as we partake of this Sacred Mystery of your Body
and Blood, draw us now into Mystic Communion with you,

May our souls rise into the immensity of Your Love; may we
perceive within ourselves Your Abiding Presence, and we come
to know that through You we are also one with all that lives,
O Thou the Giver of the Manna of Heaven, Who Lives and Reigns
in the hearts of all.

Congregation: Amen

Communion Priest

Priest: This is the Lamb of God slain ✠ from the foundation
of the world, happy are those who partake of its supper

Communion congregation

Priest: The Body of Christ and the Bread of Angels

Communicant: Amen

Priest: let us pray

Congregation: Under the Veil of earthly things now we are in communion with Christ; soon with open face shall we see Him, and being made anew like unto His own Glorious Body, may we come before Your Presence and serve You night and day.

Congregation: Amen

All: Beloved One, now let Thy servant depart in peace according to Thy Word, for mine eyes have seen Thy Salvation which Thou has prepared before the face of all people, to be a Light to Lighten the gentiles and to be the Glory of all Thy people, seekers and followers.

Priest: Unto God's Gracious Love and Protection we commit you. Christ Bless ✠ and Keeps you, Christ makes His Face to shine upon you and be Gracious unto you. Christ lifts up the Light of His Countenance upon you and gives His Peace,
Now and forever more

All: Amen

The Hymn of Yahushua

Hymn of Jesus - an esoteric explanation

This hymn can be interpreted as a ritual of initiation, performed by the master, as his disciples danced in a circle, imitating the cosmic movement and drama of creation.
The wisdom teachings are sung by the initiator in their midst, while those participants affirm the received mysteries, by the sacred word: Amen.

The dance is constructed in a circular movement, like the movements of the macrocosm and microcosm. Both realities are present and operable in different worlds (realities) where they unfold and develop.

The progression of the physical and non-physical universe, is orchestrated in a pattern of a well-ordered dance.
As one universal law states: "nothing is at rest and all vibrates", and so to appreciate this law, it should be within our nature to move (dance) according to the "song of the Universe".
It can be interpreted in such a way that this song (music of the spheres) is the perfect melody (voice) through which the cosmic Law is uttered. This is not so much a "word" in the literal sense, but a lives' expression (through movement); a bodily expression of manifesting the Heavenly law on earth and this physical existence.
Here, the holy purpose is to embody Spirit.

In this pattern of the Universe, a composition of orderly (cosmos) movement is affirmed in the Self of mankind. The Self within mankind is the total sum of all components of which the human soul (Adam Kadmon) is created, formed and made.
"One sings and dances the worlds into being"
We activate the inner planets-metals within our sphere by movement as these inner centres are moving according to the same sound (wheels).
These are actual potencies which are a microcosmic equivalent of the macrocosmic origin and are animated through certain movements and vibrations.

All these energies come together as a synthesis in the one energy
or Christ; also known as the Kabbalistic Shekinah.
And the dance should lead to this end, like after the Supper-
Communion, all are invited to dance with the Holy Spirit.

The axis in the wheel-shape within the dance, is a reference to the
eternal within the time-space-frame. Eternity can be seen as the hub of
the wheel (were all revolves around or the axis mundi) and the outer
spokes and rim are the worlds that are emanated from that Eternity.

In like manner, Christ is positioned at the centre of the wheel and
leads the ceremony as all is forthcoming from that eternal centre.
The Logos on earth; the spoken word is the expression of creation.
A song not only of praise, but a re-affirmation of creation, which
is an un-going process in the Universe.
Here we have another version of the Genesis myth, enwrapped
in a practical ceremony.
But this time not to result in the fall, but a motion of involution
and a way of initiation-evolution: a spiralling-motion up the ladder
of consciousness.
Here we answer to the call within, which is the silent voice of
initiation unto the Higher worlds.

Christ has pointed out several times that it is the soul who wishes
to create itself in the image of the Father or to be like Christ, the Anointed.
This can only be done if the soul actively and consciously
participates in the Mystery of creation and puts itself in the centre
of all things.
To surrender to the Life-stream that transforms all things, and makes
them into itself.

The soul who identifies with Christ and this alchemical fire,
they shall be transformed.
Transformation is the goal of this movement; a dance of Life,
to awaken the innermost of the Human Heart.
Importantly also is to realize that this is the way of nature: of all
things progressing along those laws which are compassionately laid
out for those who wish to see it.

Whether this song-dance is historically true or not, does not matter.
What is of great importance is that the Wisdom Teachings of All
Ages are documented and preserved for those who follow.
It is clear that the text has a definite implication and message,
but is left open for creativity in the form and expression of the dance
and movements.

At first there is the calling of the Holy Trinity: Father, Son and Holy
Spirit; Three in One.
They allude to the Primordial Triplicity of manifestation;
to understand that the One God has sacrificed itself into a pair
of masculine and feminine qualities. Without this Divine offer there
would be no division and so there would be no manifestation
of the Divine into matter.

The Rite of the Hymn of Yahushua
(Performed after communion at Maundy Thursday or within any
Eucharistic Celebration)

Priest: Glory to Thee, Father
(and we are going around in a circle)
All: Amen.

Priest: Glory to Thee, Word
All: Amen.

Priest: Glory to Thee, Grace
All: Amen.

Priest: Glory to Thee, Spirit
Glory to Thee, Holy One
Glory to Thy Glory
All: Amen.

Priest: We Praise Thee O Father
We give thanks to Thee O Light
In Whom darkness dwells not
All: Amen

Priest: For we give thanks to the Logos
I would be saved, and I would save
All: Amen.

Priest: I would be loosed, and I would loose
All: Amen.

Priest: I would be wounded and I would wound
All: Amen.

Priest: I would be begotten, and I would beget
All: Amen.

Priest: I would eat, and would be eaten
All: Amen.

Priest: I would hear, and I would be heard
All: Amen.

Priest: I would understand, and I would be understood
All: Amen.

Priest: Grace leadeth the dance; I would sing, dance you all
All: Amen.

Priest: I would play a dirge, lament you all
All: Amen.

Priest: The One - Eight sounds with us
All: Amen.

Priest: The 12th number above leadeth the dance
All: Amen.

Priest: All who's nature is to dance, doth dance
All: Amen.

Priest: Who danceth not, knows not what is being done
All: Amen.

Priest: I would flee and I would stay
All: Amen.

Priest: I would be adorn and I would adorn
All: Amen.

Priest: I would be atoned, and I would at-one
All: Amen.

Priest: I have no dwelling, and I have dwellings
All: Amen.

Priest: I have no place, and I have places
All: Amen.

Priest: I have no temples, and I have temples
All: Amen.

Priest: I am a lamp who sees me
All: Amen.

Priest: I am a mirror for those who understands me
All: Amen.

Priest: I am a door who knocks at me
All: Amen.

Priest: I am a way to thee a wayfarer
All: Amen.

Priest: Now answer to my dancing; see thyself in Me Who speaks,
And seeing what I do, keep silence on My Mysteries,
Understand by dancing what I do, for thine is the passion of man,
That I am to suffer; thou could not be conscious of what thou
dost suffer,

Were I not sent as Thy Word by the Father: I am Thy Word,
Seeing what I suffer, thou saw me as suffering,

And seeing thou didst not stand, but was moved wholly moved to be wise,
Thou hast me for a couch, rest upon me,

Who I Am, thou shalt know when I depart,
What now I Am seen to be, that I am not,

But what I Am, thou shalt see when thou comest,
I know how to suffer, thou wouldst have power not to suffer,
Know then how to suffer, and thou hast power not to suffer,

That which thou knows not, I Myself will teach You,
I am Thy God, not the betrayers,

I would be kept in time with Holy Souls,
In me know thou the Word of Wisdom,

Say thou to me again:

All: Glory to Thee Father; Glory to Thee Word; Glory to
Thee Holy Spirit.

Priest: But as for me, if thou wouldst know what I was; in a word I
Am the Word, who did play and dance all things, and was not shamed
at all.
I was Who leaped and danced,
But do thou understand all, and understanding, say:

All: Glory to Thee, Father!
And having danced these things with us, Beloved, Christ went forth.
And we, as though beside ourselves, or wakened out of a deep sleep,
fled each our separate ways.

All: Amen. Amen. Amen

Alternative liturgical Invocation
for Communion

A.S.A. APOSTOLIC SUCCESSION OF ARIMATHEA

After Agnus Dei and omitting "Christ our Passover...."

Priest: Behold My Beloved,
I have shown you the power of silence,
how thoroughly it heals and how pleasing it is unto God.
Therefore I have written to you to show yourselves,
and be strong in this work that you have undertaken.
That you may know that it is by silence that the Saints grow,
By silence that the Power of God dwells in them,
And through silence that the Mysteries of God,
Are more made known unto them.

All: Amen

Communion (post communio)

Priest: And Melchizedek King of Salem, brought forth Bread and Wine,
and he was Priest of the Most High God. And like unto Joseph of
Arimathea he gave the Blessing of Heaven so he might live.
He Blessed them all and said:
Blessed be my faithful companions of the Most High God, Beloved
of Heaven and Earth.

Body of Christ and the Bread of Angels ✠ Blood of Christ and Grail
of Eternal Life

All: Amen

Christ's Prayer

O Cosmic Birther of all radiance and vibration, soften the ground of our being and carve out a space within us where Your Presence can abide.

Fill us with Your creativity so that we may be empowered to bear the fruits of Your mission.

Let each of our actions bear fruit in accordance with our desire. Endow us with the Wisdom to produce and share what each being needs to grow and flourish.

Untie the tangled threads of destiny that bind us, as we release others from the entanglement of past mistakes.

Do not let us be seduced by that which would divert us from our true purpose, but illuminate the opportunities of the present moment.

For Thou are the ground and the fruitful vision; the birth, power, and fulfillment, as all is gathered and made whole once again through You.

And so it is and shall always be.

Amen

Invocation of the Angel of Christ

"Let us invoke the Angel of Christ Masemariah, the one who is like Christ; who opens the Veil of Heaven,

You who stand before the Holy of Holies and reveals to us the endless realm of Divinity,

You and the Son of God are brothers and companions, rending the Veil between the uncreated Light and the world,

For those who are ready to receive, let them come upon the mountain, or enter the temple,

Speaking thy Name - MASEMARIAH who holds the 72 Names of God,

And who is the ultimate Guardian on the threshold, barring the way for those who are not purified,

Opening the Way for others who have become a luminous mirror for the Light of the Holy One"

Part 2 Sacral rites of preparation & purification

Rite of Admission

A.S.A. APOSTOLIC SUCCESSION OF ARIMATHEA

To be used when the sacraments of Baptism and Confirmation have
already been received elsewhere. If they have not been previously
received, then the administration of those Sacraments constitutes full
membership of the A.S.A.

This rite may precede Mass or take place instead of the sermon /
meditation during Mass or follow after Mass.
It may also be held as a separate ceremony, in which it is always
followed by the rite of Holy Communion. Only a priest may confer
this Rite of Admission.

The Rite
(Priest goes to stand before the altar invoking)

In the Name of God, the Creator + the Redeemer + and
the Sanctifying + Spirit

Congregation: Amen

(Priest faces the candidate and congregation)

Dearly beloved, we stand in the House of Christ, at the centre of the
Universe. Here, before God the Omnipresent and all the Holy Angels
of Heaven, we call before us N.... who would be admitted into
the Apostolic Succession of Arimathea and therefore following
the Way of Christ. Becoming a fellow traveller and pilgrim,
we are happy to welcome you into this circle of compassion and love.

(The candidate comes forward, bows to the altar)

Candidate: Adsum, I am present. Reverend Father / Mother, I desire
to be admitted into the community of the Apostolic Succession
of Arimathea and follow the Way of Christ

Priest: Will you endeavour to live in the Spirit of Compassion towards all humanity and all living beings, striving to overcome selfishness and seeking to extend God's Light?

Candidate: I will, so help me God

Priest: Will you seek to manifest in your thoughts, words and deeds, the power of God which indwells you?

Candidate: I will, so help me God

Priest: Is it true that you are seeking the Christ-within and wish to serve creation?

Candidate: Such is my desire, so help me God

Priest: May God, the Fountain of all Holiness keep you in all these resolves and strengthen you in all Goodness, Beauty and Truth + Let us pray (candidate kneels before priest who places one end of the stole upon the candidate's shoulder and offers the following prayer while candidate looks into the Shroud)
O Christ our Risen Master, receive your servant N.... who desires to be united with You. Through Your Bride, the Shekinah and our Temple, Sanctify + this soul (name) with Heavenly Grace, so that by bringing forth the fruits of the Spirit, she / he may be made anew, like unto Your own Glorious Body and attain the Treasures of the Kingdom of Heaven.

All: O Christ, Beloved Master within the Hearts of Humanity, to You be Praise and Adoration forevermore.

Congregation: Amen

Candidate: Amen and Peace to all Beings

Holy Communion follows & Sacred Blessing

Priest: Our help is in the Name of God

All: Who has made Heaven and Earth

Priest: Blessed are the pure of Heart

All: For they shall see God

Priest (taking up the Cross) The Blessing of God Almighty -
the Father + the Son + and the Holy + Spirit descend upon you (cross
on forehead) and remain with you always

All: Amen. Amen. Amen

Sacrament of Baptism

A.S.A. APOSTOLIC SUCCESSION OF ARIMATHEA

The priest makes Holy water in the usual way and then says
the additional prayer over it before the arrival of the baptised.
Requirements: a container for the Baptismal waters (font) a small
jug, shell or cruet (to poor water over candidates forehead),
a white candle, oil of the catechumens and a white scarf or kerchief.
Priest is vested in Alb and white stole.

The Rite

Priest: In the Name of the Father, the ✟ Son and the Holy Spirit.
Creator, Redeemer and Transforming Spirit.

Congregation: Amen

The Presentation

(If the candidate is a child (s)he is presented by the sponsors
or god-parents)
Candidate or Sponsor: Reverend Father / Mother, we present to you this
child, praying that you will receive this child into the Fellowship of Christ.

(If the candidate is an adult (s)he presents her / himself):
Candidate: Reverend Father / Mother, I present myself as a child
of God, praying that you will receive me into the Fellowship
of Christ and the Apostolic Succession of Arimathea.

(Priest addresses all present (for a child))
Christ, the Holy Child of Light, in His great Compassion for
humanity, has willed that His mystical Bride, the Shekinah and our
Temple, should guide and protect those entrusted to Her, through
every transition in their incarnate lives - from the cradle to the grave.
This is why the Sacrament of Baptism was ordained; a rite to which
Christ submitted, so that our Holy Temple may welcome and give
protective blessings to the one who has newly entered the earth.

Let us pray and bless this pilgrim who has come to make its journey
as a passer-by and servant of God. Let this body be purified from any
stains of corruption or evil, becoming sanctified as a vehicle for their
Immortal Spirit and for the service of the Divine, Who is the Source
of all Life. So I ask to join your prayers to mine in this Holy Rite by
which this child will become a member of Christ's Mystical Body
and receive the protection of Heaven.

(for an adult)
Christ, the Holy Child of Light, in His great Compassion for
humanity, has willed that His Mystical Bride, the Shekinah and our
Temple, should guide and protect those entrusted to Her through
every transition in their incarnate lives; from the cradle to the grave.
This is why the Sacrament of Baptism was ordained; a rite to which
Christ submitted, so that our Holy Temple may welcome and give
protective blessings to the one who wishes to become a living
member in the Fellowship of Christ and the followers of the Way.
May (s)he share in the communion with our Ancestors and Saints.
Let us pray for this soul and bless this pilgrim who has come to make
its journey as a passer-by and servant of God. Let this body be
purified from any stains of corruption or evil, becoming sanctified as
a vehicle for their immortal Spirit and for the service of the Divine,
Who is the Source of all Life. So I ask to join your prayers to mine
in this Holy Rite by which this woman / man will become a member
of Christ's Mystical Body and receive the protection of Heaven,

A person so appointed may now read from the Gospels:

Reader: the Holy Gospel according to Mark
They brought young children to Christ that He should touch them, and
His disciples rebuked those that brought them. But when Jesus saw it,
He was much displeased and said unto them: "Allow the little children
to come unto Me and forbid them not, for such is the Kingdom of God.
I say unto you, whosoever shall not receive the Kingdom of God as a
little child, they shall not enter therein". And He took them up in His
arms, put His hands upon them and blessed them.

(Priest places his / her hand on the head of the candidate)
Priest: let us pray

All: Powerful and ever-present God, Whose power flows in every
living creature, You Who are the font of all Life and Goodness, direct
upon this Your child, a ray of Your clear Light and blessing.
Purge all blindness of heart, break any chains of iniquity by which
(s)he may be bound. Open to her / him the Gate of Your Glory, so
that being replenished by Your Spirit, this soul may grow in Holiness
and Wisdom and joyfully walk the path You have appointed for her /
him. Through Christ, the ideal human stature.

Congregation: Amen.

The Exorcism

Priest: In the Name which is above every Name and in the Power of
the ✝ Father and the Son ✝ and of the Holy Spirit ✝, I exorcise all
influences and seeds of evil. I lay upon them the Spell of Christ's
Presence, that they trouble not this child of God.

(Hand on the back of the head of the candidate)
Priest: For it is Christ, the One of Compassion who has called you now
to Divine Grace and Blessing through the still waters of Baptism.

Priest: EMPHATHA - Open Thyself ✝ (silence). Let your mind and
heart be opened to the Holy Spirit and the Heavenly World, so that
your entire nature may be dedicated to Divine service. May you
be receptive to the Heavenly Will and your body become pure like
the Temple of God.

(Hand now extended over the candidate)
Priest: O God of Hosts, let Your ever-abiding Power come over this
Your servant, now dedicated to Your Service that (s)he may receive
the fullness of the new birth through Christ and all the Holy Angels
of Heaven.

Congregation: Amen.

(Priest now places one end of the stole on the candidates shoulder)
Priest: Come into the Temple of God so that with Christ you shall
inherit Peace Profound and Eternal Life.

The Anointing

(Priest moistens her / his thumb with the oil of Catechumens,
then without touching the candidate, makes the sign of the cross,
one in front and one behind the candidate)

Priest: In the Name of Christ in all the worlds, I anoint you with oil
for your protection. May your Holy Angel go before ✠ you
and follow ✠ you, may your Angel be with you in your sitting and
in your rising, by night and by day....

(Priest anoints the top of the head of the candidate)
Priest: May your Angel go before you in your going ✠ out and your
coming ✠ in, and keep you in all your ways.

Congregation: Amen.

(Priest now pours Baptismal waters 3 times over the head of
the candidate)

Priest: (name) I baptize you in the Name of the Father ✠ and
of the Son ✠ and of the Holy Spirit ✠. Creator, Redeemer
and Transforming Spirit.

Congregation: Amen.

(Priest places hand on candidate's head)

Priest: Be you closed ✠

(Candidate is now given the white kerchief)

Priest: Take this burning Light, kindled from God's own Altar,
as a sign of the Ever-burning Light of your Immortal Spirit.
May you every grow in the Knowledge of the Divine Light that
abides in your heart, your mind and your incarnate body.
Remember you are the Light. May you forever shine!

The Charge

Priest: Hear the words of Christ - Thou shalt love thy God with all
your heart and with all your soul and with all thy mind and thy
strength. This is the first and great commandment, and the second is
like unto it - you shall love your neighbour as thyself. On these two
commandments hang all the laws and the prophets. Having today
been baptized and now being a member of the Mystical Body
of Christ, in due time come before this Council if you so wish
and be confirmed in the Holy Spirit.

(If the candidate wishes to be adopted in the A.S.A.)

Priest: May I welcome you O beautiful one, who came to enter
this new life and walk the Way of Christ. You are now adopted into
the spiritual family and lineage of the Apostolic Succession
of Arimathea. The pure Teachings of Christ are leading us on.
There is no other authority but Christ on our path and only your own
vow to God is binding you. May we share the Love and Light of
Christ as companions in this Spiritual Work.

Closing

Priest: (name) Go in ✞ Peace and Grace and walk with God,
wherefore no evil shall touch you.

Congregation: Amen

Sacrament of Confirmation

A.S.A. APOSTOLIC SUCCESSION OF ARIMATHEA

Requirements: Holy Chrism and lavabo bowl & cloth. Priest needs a towel, a chair before the altar, and an assistant. Recipients should be 12 years or older who may choose another name (conformation name). Candidates should be informed about the ritual (rehearsed). Priest is dressed in white with white or red stole.

The Rite

Priest: In the Name of God, the Creator, the Redeemer ✣ and the Transforming Spirit.

Congregation: Amen.

(Priest sits before the altar addressing the candidate(s) concerning the Holy Spirit of God that is to be imparted in this Sacrament. When the address is completed, the candidate(s) stand(s) for the interrogation.)

The Interrogation

Priest: Will you seek to live in the Spirit of Compassion with all humanity and with all life?

Candidate: I will, so help me God.

Priest: Will you strife to express in your thoughts, words and deeds the Divine Power which shall be given to you on this day?

Candidate: I will, so help me God. (candidate kneels)

Priest: May the Blessing ✣ of the Holy Spirit come down upon you and may the Power of the Most High keep you in all your ways.

All: Amen.

(Priest and all others kneel as they sing the Veni Creator)

Come Thou Creator, Spirit Blest and in our souls take Thy rest
Come with Thy Grace and Heavenly aid, to fill the hearts which
Thou Hast made,

Great Paraclete, to Thee we cry, O Highest Gift of God Most High
O Living Fount, O Fire, O Love, and sweet anointing from above,

Thou in Thy Sevenfold Gift art known, Thee finger of Gods hand
we own The promise of the Father, Thou Who dost the tongue with
power endow,

Kindle out senses from above and make our hearts overflow with love
With patience firm and virtue high, the weakness of our flesh supply,

Far let us drive our tempting foe and shine abiding peace bestow
So shall we not with for guide, turn from the path of life aside,

O may Thy Grace on us bestow, the Father and the Son to know
Thee to endless time confessed of both Eternal Spirit Blessed,

All Glory while the ages run, be to the Father and to the Son
Who gave us Life the same to Thee, O Holy Spirit, Eternally.

Congregation: Amen

(All are now seated. Each candidate to be confirmed is now brought
to kneel before the bishop and places his / her hands palm to palm
between those of the Priest)

Candidate: Most reverend father, I offer myself to be a warrior
of the Light in Service of the Divine

Priest: In Christ's All-Holy Name do I accept you

(Taking Chrism upon his thumb and placing his hand upon
the candidate's head, the priest-bishop draws on the forehead the sign
of the Cross)

Priest: I have received authority from the successors of Christ's
Apostles and especially Joseph of Arimathea and the followers of
The Way. I say now unto you: (new name) receive the Holy Spirit for
the Glory of God and the perfecting of humanity. So I sign you with
the Light of the Cross and confirm you with the Chrism of Salvation.
In the Name of the Father ✠ and the Son ✠ and the Holy Spirit ✠

Congregation: Amen

Priest: Therefore (new name) go forth into the world in the Name
of Christ, and be an example on your path.

(Priest lightly touches the left cheek of the candidate and hot wax
from a candle is received in the left palm of the candidate's hand.)

Priest: PAX TECUM - PEACE BE WITH YOU

(Candidate reverences the Shroud and returns to his / her seat and
when all have received the Sacrament)

Priest: My Children in Christ, having now received the Sacred Gift
of God's Holy Spirit, keep the vehicles of your bodies ever clean and
clear, as befits a temple of the Most High God, and a channel for so
great a power. Understand and remember this, and keep that channel
open, by living a life of selfless service, so will the Divine Life that
is within you, shine forth in ever greater glory and abundance.

(Priest rises and extends his / her hands towards the confirmed)

Priest: O Christ, our master and teacher, you gave your Holy Spirit to
your Apostles, requesting that they and their successors should
impart that same Spirit to the rest of God's people, we give thanks
that your Will has been fulfilled in this your servant(s) here on this
day within the company and companionship of Joseph of Arimathea
and the Grail Bearers.

We commend to your protection this soul, who has now been
confirmed in the Spirit, may (s)he / they so bear themselves as
faithful warriors of the Light in the temple here on earth.

That they may come to stand before you and the Shining Hosts of Heaven. Hear our prayer O Great King of Glory to Whom is offered praise and service by the Holy Angels.

Congregation: Amen.

The Blessing

Priest: Our help ✠ is in the Name of God

All: Who has made Heaven and Earth

Priest: Blessed are the Pure of Heart

All: For they shall see God

Priest: The Blessing of God Almighty - the Father ✠ the Son ✠ and the Holy ✠ Spirit descend upon you and remain with you.

Congregation: Amen

Sacrament of Confession & Absolution

Generally speaking, the Absolution given during Mass is sufficient
for most transgressions and one may prayerfully hear Mass with
intention of availing oneself of Divine Clemency. However,
an individual may feel the need for private confession to avail
themselves of spiritual counsel from the priest.
It is important that the priest endeavours to function from a Christ-
like state of unconditional love. It should be impressed upon
the penitent that Absolution does not mitigate the Law of Karma,
but it does strengthen the recipient with Grace to restore the balance
and be restored to a state of spiritual health. True penitence is not
some grovelling in the mire or abasement. That is the state of one
who persists in sinfulness. Penitence is an indication of spiritual
maturity, taking stock of one's shortcomings and resolving to try
to do better in the future.
This Sacrament may be administered in any suitable place. The priest
is usually seated to represent judgement and wears a violet stole.

The Rite

Priest: In the Name of the Creator + the Redeemer + and
the Transforming + Spirit.

All: Amen

Penitent: O most Holy One, You have created me to be immortal
and made me to be an image of your own Eternity, yet often I forget
the glory of my heritage and wander from the path that leads to
wholeness. But You Oh God has made me for Yourself, while I am
ever restless until I find Peace in You.
Look with the eyes of Your Love upon my manifold imperfections
and pardon all my shortcomings, so that I may be filled with the
Brightness of your Everlasting Light and become the unspotted
mirror of Your Power and the image of Your Goodness, through
Christ the Indwelling Light.

All: Amen

Priest: May Christ be in your + heart and on your + lips so that you may make a good confession

(Priest presents Shroud to penitent who lays both hands in prayer on the Shroud)

Penitent: I confess to the Almighty God and to you my confessor, that I have sinned, and made wrong decisions and caused ill effects in my life, especially I have.... for these and all my other offences which I cannot remember at this very moment. I am heartily sorry and will endeavour to rectify myself, asking absolution of you my confessor, in the Name of God + and the benefit of the Spiritual Counsel.

(Priest gives such counsel as is needed for the penitent. The advice is bound by the will of the penitent and the priest gives a moral and metaphysical counsel based upon spiritual values. Absolution is given so that the penitent is released from guilt and shame and may work on her / his inner and outer path and the restoration and healing needed for progression from this moment on.)

Absolution

Priest: Christ our Supreme Teacher, Who gave power to this Temple and Church to forgive the sins of those who turn their faces back to the Light of God. From this tender Compassion I forgive you all your transgressions, and by the Authority of Christ, committed unto me, I + absolve you from all your sins, in the Name of the Father + and of the Son + and of the Holy Spirit +

All: Amen

Priest: Be open. Emphata. Go in peace and walk your path under the protection of Heaven and be guided by the Heavenly Hosts, and may you continuously pray in the Presence of the Holy One +

All: Amen

Solemn Benediction with anointing of the Sick

A.S.A. APOSTOLIC SUCCESSION OF ARIMATHEA

Required:
Altar: central candle and 12 candles, corporeal for Monstrance
and pyx or ciborium containing the Sacrament. Vessel with oil for
the sick. Veiled monstrance placed and the side of the altar
Sanctuary: Holy water and Aspergil, thurible with charcoal &
incense, lavabo jug and towel, humeral veil
Minister: priest vested in Alb, stole (straight down), pectoral cross,
pontifical ring and staff (crosier). At least one assistant present in
white Alb (candles and charcoal are lit before the rite commences)
Soft background music is optional

The Rite

(Having reached the altar and genuflected, the priest gives the Invocation)

In the Name of God, the + Creator, the + Redeemer and
the Transforming + Spirit

All: Amen

Aspergil

Priest: May all be purified by Heaven's Dew to receive this
Sacrament of Holy Unction, and we pray that the Divine may send
the Healing Angels of Light, so that all may be restored to health
of mind, body and soul

All: Amen

All: (kneel and say)
Create in me a clean heart. O Forgiving Love, and renew a right
Spirit within me.

Here is my body, I cast it down before You, heal its imperfections
with Your perfection and make me whole
Here is my mind, I spread it out before You, forgive my foolishness
and ignorance with Your Bright Wisdom
Here is my heart, it is Yours alone, forgive its restless wanderings
from You
Here is my life, I offer it unto You, do with me as You will, forgive me,
Together with Yourself, restore unto me, the Joy of Your Salvation,
That I may awake in Your likeness and be satisfied, through Christ,
the Indwelling Light,
Amen

Absolution

Priest: The Mercy and Grace of God be upon you + will forgive all
your sins and bring us to Eternal Light

All: Amen

(All remain kneeling (priest kneels again) while assistant unveils
Monstrance turning to face the congregation. Then collecting the
thurible and incense and assistant kneels beside priest. Priest puts
incense unto the coal and takes thurible. In kneeling position bow to
Monstrance. Rising, the priest incenses the enthroned sacrament with
three swings and gently keeps incensing with the following hymn)

O Salutaris Hostia

All sing - O Salutaris Hostia

O saving Victor opening wide, the Gate of Heaven to us below
Our foes press in from every side, Thine aid supply, Thy strength bestow

All praise and thanks to Thee ascend, forevermore blest One-in-Three
O grant us life that shall not end, in our true native land with Thee
Amen

(After a moment of silence an appointed servant reads)

Reader: Hear the words from the Apostle James

Is any sick among you? Let them call for the priest of this Temple and
let them pray for the sick, anointing them with oil in the Name of God.
And the prayer of faith shall save the sick and God shall raise them up.
If transgressions have been committed, they shall be forgiven.
Pray for one another that you may be healed, for the fervent prayer
of the righteous shall be heard and bring us to a greater wholeness.

Priest: Let us pray to God, the Compassionate and the Merciful One,
to send the Holy Spirit for the Healing of the sick

All: sing Veni Creator

Veni Creator

Come, Holy Spirit, Creator Blest
and in our souls take up Thy rest
come with Thy Grace and Heavenly aid
to fill the hearts which Thou hast made
O comforter, to Thee we cry
O Heavenly Gift of God Most High
O fount of Life and Fire of Love
and Sweet Anointing from above

Thou in Thy Sevenfold Gifts are known
Thou, finger of God's hand we own
Thou, promise of the Father, Thou
Who dost the tongue with power imbue

Kindle our sense from above
and make our hearts overflow with love
with patience firm and virtue high
the weakness of our flesh supply

Far from us drive the foe we dread
and grant us Thy peace instead
so shall we not, with Thee for guide
turn from the path of life aside

Oh, may Thy Grace on us bestow
the Father and the Son to know
and Thee, through endless times confessed
of both the Eternal Spirit Blest

Now to the Father and the Son
Who rose from death, be glory given
with Thou, O Holy Comforter
henceforth by all in earth and heaven.
Amen

(All may now be seated. Priest stands before altar while assistant
collects oil for the sick. All who desires healing may come forward,
one at the time, genuflecting before the Sacrament and kneel before
the priest)

Priest: By the Ineffable Name of God, in the Power of the Father +
and the Son + and the Holy + Spirit, I exorcise all evil influences
that they depart and trouble not this Child of God

(Priest puts some Holy Oil on the thumb and anoints forehead)
Priest: By the Radiant Power of Christ and invoking the help of
the Holy Archangel Raphael, I + anoint you with Oil for the healing
of the Soul, mind and body

(In silence the priest proceeds to anoint in the same manner as before
the centre at the top of the head, throat and the nape of the neck.
With full intention to act as God's healing instrument, the priest
places both hands on the person's head)

Priest: Christ the Anointed of God, outpours this healing power upon
you and enfold you in Light Divine.

Congregation: Amen

Priest: All are now welcome to receive these Mysteries from the altar
of the Beloved, for all His Children are most welcome

Communion

Body of Christ and the Bread of Angels + Blood of Christ,
Grail of Eternal Life +

(All kneel or sit down in silent adoration)

(Priest puts incense on coal in thurible and swings while all sing)

Tantum Ergo Sacramentum

Therefore we before Him bending, this great Sacrament revere
Types and shadows have their ending, for the newer rite is here
Faith our outward sense befriending, makes our inward vision clear
Glory let us give a Blessing, to the Father and the Son
Honour, Might and Praise addressing, while Eternal ages run
Ever too Her Love confessing, who from both with both is One
Amen

Priest: Thou didst give them Bread from Heaven

All: Containing within itself all Sweetness and Grace

Priest: O Christ Thou Hidden Dweller in the human heart

All: Open your eyes in us, that we may see

Priest: O God in this wonderful Sacrament of the altar, You have
given us a Living Memorial of Your Endless Love for humanity
and all creation

Let us venerate the Sacred Mystery of Your Body and Blood, that
we may always see within us the Power of Your Indwelling Life
So by the glad outpouring of our lives in service, we may know
ourselves to be One with Thee and through Thee with all that lives
One God throughout the ages of ages

All: Amen

Priest: To the Mystery of the Holy Trinity - Father, Son + and Holy
Spirit, Three-in-One,
To the Christ, Son of the Great Light and the Prince of Peace
To the Seven Mighty Archangels before the Throne and to the Holy
Assembly of Just Humans made perfect, the Watchers, the Saints,
and the Holy Ones.
Be praise unceasing to every living creature, now and forevermore

All: Amen

(Priest makes cross with the Monstrance while assistant rings
the bells. If another assistant is present the Monstrance is incensed
during the crossing and blessing of the people. Then, Sacrament
is veiled and procession is going out of the temple.
All remain in profound silence) ⚧

Sacrament of Matrimony

A.S.A. APOSTOLIC SUCCESSION OF ARIMATHEA

Both bride and bridegroom are sitting before the altar, while priest opens the ceremony

Priest: In the Name of God, the Creator + the Redeemer + and the Transforming + Spirit

All: Amen

Priest: We are gathered in this place or temple of the Most Holy One, where dwells Peace, Blessing and Lovingkindness. May we welcome these two souls who wish to commit themselves not only to each other, but to sanctify their lives in the eternal connection with the Holy Spirit

Is there any soul present who would be against this union?
(short silence)

Priest: Then I absolve you all, in the name of the most Holy One, so that you are clean and pure and your life may dwell in the Light Eternal +

All: Come and let us gather together with these souls

(Priest performs Asperges - three times self, three times the altar and three times the congregation)

(Priest performs Asperges Three times couple)

Priest: Only through water and fire shall you enter the Kingdom of Heaven; only when you make the male into female and the female into the male shall you see the manifestation of Heaven.

All: Amen

Priest: Let the rings come forward (someone presents the rings on a platter or tray, and the priest sprinkles them with Holy Water)

Priest: True Faith and an ever-deepening Love is now a part of your
union, wearing these rings you will always be remembered of this
Sacred vow to each other and the Holy Spirit within you

All: Amen

(Priest holding the rings in front of the bride and bridegroom)
Priest: Breathe upon these rings and remember that your Breath
is the Breath of the Holy Spirit (both blow over the rings)

Priest: Let the father or guardian of the Bride come forward....
(Bride is taken by the right arm and guided to the priest, who hands
her over to the bridegroom)

Saying: Receive the precious gift of God

All: Amen

Priest: Bridegroom, repeat after me: In the Name of Christ within all
creation, I swear that I shall serve my Lady as she is the representative
of the Divine on earth

Priest: Bride, repeat after me: In the Name of Christ within all
Creation, I swear that I shall serve Christ as he is the guardian
of the Divine on earth

All: Amen and Peace to these souls

(Priest stands before the Bride and Bridegroom in front of the altar)
Priest: Please repeat after me this solemn obligation:

Priest & Bridegroom: I take thee to be my wedded wife, to have and
to hold from this day forward, for better, for worse, for richer and
poorer, in sickness and in health, to love, to cherish and to honour till
death us here do part; and thereunto in the Presence of God, the Holy
One and in the Power and Love of Christ our Teacher and Master,
I plight Thee my vow and loyalty.

All: Amen, so it will be

(Priest stand before the Bride and Bridegroom in front of the altar
and says to the bride)
Priest: please repeat after me this solemn obligation

Priest & Bride: I take thee to be my wedded husband, to have and to
hold from this day forward, for better, for worse, for richer and
poorer, in sickness and in health, to love, to cherish and to honour till
death us here do part; and thereunto in the Presence of God, the Holy
One and in the Power and Love of Christ our Teacher and Master,
I plight Thee my vow and loyalty.

All: Amen, so it will be

Placing of the Rings

Priest: Come together in this our Holy Place and unite your presence
with each other

(Rings are taken by the priest; first the Bridegroom takes ring and counts
the first three finger of the Bride: thumb, index finger and middle finger)

Bridegroom: In the Name of the Creator, Redeemer and
Transforming Spirit
(putting on the ring).... With this ring Thee I wed, my truest love
I thee pledge, with my body I give thee reverence and with my
strength I will shield thee.

All: Amen

(Bride takes the ring and counts the finger of the Bridegroom: thumb,
index finger and middle finger)

Bride: In the Name of the Creator, Redeemer and Transforming
Spirit (putting on the ring).... With this ring Thee I wed, my truest
love I thee pledge, with my body I give thee reverence and with my
strength I will shield thee.

All: Amen

Unction

(Priest touches the heads of Bride and Bridegroom with Holy Oil)
Priest: I join you in marriage; the sacred union or Hieros Gamos,
in the Name of the Father, the Son + and the Holy Spirit

All: Amen

(The hands of the Bride and Bridegroom are put together; stole
and right hand of the priest goes over their hands)
Priest: Those whom God hath joined together, let no man seek
to put asunder.

All: Amen

Priest: May you seal this union with the Kiss of Christ on each other's
lips and offer each other the Life of the Spirit (kiss is exchanged)

Priest: (priest turns towards the people) Let us pray for these two
souls who have turned towards the Light in one another

Priest: O Eternal God, Creator and Preserver of all mankind, giver of
all Spiritual Grace, the author of everlasting life; send Thy Blessing
upon these Thy servants; this woman and this man (or of similar sex)
whom we bless in Thy Name. May these souls surely perform and
keep the vow and covenant betwixt them made, and may so hold their
lives in the knowledge and love of Thee, that they may dwell together
in Holy Love and Peace. Through Christ, the indwelling Light.

All: Amen

Priest: Father of Light from Whose Hands all souls come into
the world, do Thou Bless the Marriage of these Thy servants with
Fruitfulness and Thy Grace raining down upon them.

All: May their lives be so Sanctified in Thy service that this bondage will
radiate Eternal Blessing upon their lives and upon all those they meet.
(All raise their hands in gesture of blessing)

Priest: Almighty God pours upon you both the Riches of Heaven, Sanctify and Bless you, that your life from this day on becomes truly a Heaven on earth.

All: Amen, so mote it be in all the years to come

Burial rite of the dead

The first and foremost importance of a funeral rite is to guide
the liberated soul and surround it with peace and spiritual power.
The offering of the Holy sacrifice for the repose of the soul is
important in the preparations. The other part of the rite consists
of hallowing and consecrating the grave or place of transition.
The latter is also about giving assurance and comfort to the relatives
and friends. If this is a burial of the clergy the staff and missal
Chalice of the departed will be included in the coffin, if they
are not passed on to someone else.

The priest and clergy ask the people not to hinder the departed with
unhappiness and grief throughout the service.

Priest: In the Name of God, the Creator + the Redeemer + and
the Transforming + Spirit

All: Amen

Priest invokes:
Companions of the Light, we are gathered here today to celebrate
the passing into the Higher Life of our dear Sister / Brother (name)
It is but natural that we who have known and loved this soul, should
regret this departure from amongst us. Yet, on this occasion it is our
duty to think not of ourselves but of the soul (name) and her / his
spiritual journey.
Therefore must we strenuously endeavour to lay aside the thought of our
personal loss and dwell only upon the passing from this life to the next.

All: Amen and praise be unto (name of the passing soul)

Priest: Let us chant the Sacred Name of Christ (YHVH) and sing the
fullness of this soul into being, the Eternal Life and Being of (name)

(Priest performs Asperges - the coffin three times)
Priest: Only through water and fire shall you enter the Kingdom of Heaven

Priest: All Encompassing One, Who ceaselessly creates and sustains,
The fabric of the Universe, send forth Your Holy and Beloved Angels,
To guard, encourage, protect and teach all who dwell within this place
In Your strength O God, do we command all adverse powers, to
wither into nothingness, that they shall not abide, and that our
temples ☩ within, and our temples ☩ without, may emerge as strong,
pure vessels, to contain the Eternal Mystery, as it unfolds on earth

Purification (censing)

Priest: Purify this temple of (name) O God, so that the true vehicle
may come forth and liberate itself from this earthly body, growing
into the fullness of Christ, a Temple of Living Stones, through which
Infinite Life may flow. Let the Angels and Archangels join us in this
Work of transforming the Earth

All: Amen

Priest: Grant that this soul may rest in Thy Eternity
Congregation: And let perpetual Light shine upon this soul
Priest: Come forth to meet (name) O ye Angels of Heaven
Congregation: Receive (name) into Your Fellowship and
Company of Light
Priest: May the Choirs of Angels receive this soul
Congregation: And guide and protect towards Eternal Peace
Priest: Grant this soul a fluent transition following its destiny
Congregation: And let Light and Grace shine throughout
the journey homewards

Priest: O God in whose unspeakable love the souls of the departed find
rest and peace. In Thy Name we absolve (name) from every bond of
sin; this Thy servant who has cast off this garment of flesh. May Thy
Holy Angels bear this soul in their tender care, so that the Gates of
Heaven open and the path that lies further may be revealed. Let Christ
come to stand before this soul and bring Peace and Guidance.

All: Amen, let us open the Gates before Christ

(Holy Communion is an option at this point in the rite)

Priest: (presents the Shroud to the coffin and the people)
Behold My Face after the resurrection and the rising from the tomb
after my physical death. I have laid down my temporal appearance
so you can all see Me. I Am That I AM.

(Shroud is put over the Mass Chalice or over the Altar)

All: May our companion and beloved soul behold Thy Face now
and forever more. Amen

Priest: Almighty God Who has dominion over both the living
and the dead, and Who holds all of creation in the everlasting arms
and embrace of Love, we pray Thee for the Peace and repose of this
Your servant (name), fading out of this earthly world, but ever-living
unto Thee. The journey ahead is therefore marked by Your Blessing
and Light.

All: Through Christ our Beloved Master and Guide

Priest: Likewise O Christ, we pray Thee for those who love
Thy servant, those whom Thou hast called to sacrifice the solace
of its earthly presence. Comfort all those present here with
Thy Lovingkindness, and strengthened by Thee, resting upon
Thy Wisdom they may put aside their sorrow and grief, so that we
all can pour upon our beloved companion (name) all thoughts
and intentions of Love, Grace and Beauty.

All: Amen

(The coffin is now taken to its final place, where it is sprinkled again
with holy water and purified with incense)

Priest: In the Name of the Most Holy One, we commit the cast-off
body of this dear and beloved soul (name) who will be brought back
to the Good Earth (or the Fires of Heaven).

Earth to earth, ashes to ashes, dust to dust; so shall this body of
the world return to its proper place, but we know that the soul travels
from Light to Light, always remembering the Divine Presence,
transmigrating from body to body.
Let us remember too that we were called forth, created, formed
and made because we are Loved and we live because we are Loved,
but we will also see death because we are Loved. The Angel of Death
is also the Angel of Love and of Endless Compassion.

All: We have faith in the Light which is our True Being

Priest: Blessed are those who die in the arms of Christ for they
are loved forever +

All: Those who passed through the gates of death with Christ are
born again in Spirit

Priest: The souls of the righteous are in the hand of God and no pain
or suffering will be their part. In the sight of the unwise we all seem
to perish after death, and there is no Light but only darkness and
destruction. God created the soul to be immortal in the image of its
own Eternity. God sits above life and death together with us and each
and every one of us resides next to the Throne of the Mighty and
Beloved One, held in Peace and nurtured by God's Infinite Blessings.
The Heavens are stretched like a canopy while the earth is planted for
the soul to pass through. Remember all of us, you descendants
of the Most Holy One, that we are passerby and that this world
is a doorway and not the resting place of our soul. Our Home is
the Presence of Christ and our refuge lies there where we find
the Father +, the Son + and the Holy Spirit +
O Father of Light in Who there is no darkness, fill our hearts with
Peace coming from Thy Angels who sing their beautiful Hymns to us

All: They sing to the departing soul and to the faithful ones here present

Priest: O Thou the great Giver of all Life, we understand that without
death, the cycle of Love is not completed, and that we need to
surrender unto Thy Graceful touch. Let us trust in Thy Providence
and abide in the knowledge of our immortal soul.

May we on this journey be received by Christ and our inner teacher
who hast helped and aided us throughout our lives.
In lovingkindness and humility we bow (all bow) for this soul (name)
who receives our blessing and reassuring smile at this Sacred
Moment, initiated by the Most Holy One, Who is our help in Life
and Death. Christ open our Hearts - EMPATHA!

All: We open up to Thee. So will it be, now and forever more

(With the descending of the coffin all people sing the Kadosh chant
with the priest)

Priest: May we all depart in Peace according to Thy Word
and receive Thy comfort now and in the days to come.

All: Blessing and Peace to the dead and the living. Amen

Warding of the Sacred Circle

(Candles: two upon the altar or if preferred at each quarter
of the temple. Holy Water and charcoal ready in a vessel.
Priest vests in Alb and Stole & wears cross, colour white)

The Rite

(Priest kneels before the altar)

Priest: Adsum Domine, here I am Christ, grant me the power
to extend Thy Light, Here I am Christ, Bless me in service with
Spiritual Sight,
Here I am Christ, awaken within me Thy Holy Might,
The Indwelling Light said unto me: Behold! Thou art my chosen
servant, my gift of the earth,
Before the stars were born, thou were in my Womb, thy soul was
sealed to me for all time,
Thou art my Sacred hand upon the world, my instrument of Light,
Joy and Grace,
To thee I give the Breath of Spirit's Power, the awesome Secrets
of Heaven, Paradise and Hell,
I give thee all these Gifts that thou may know my Love,
Use all in service for the ease of man and beast, be a cleansing fire
to purify corruption,
A pool of Peace to bring surcease of thy pain, and keep close
within thy heart all Wisdom given,

Safe and sacred within thy Holy Temple, with consecrated hands
make whole the broken,
With consecrated soul, reach out and give this creation my Peace

All: Here I am Christ, all my talents at Thy feet I lay,
Here I am Christ, Thou art the One creator of all things,
Here I am Christ, Thou art the Omnipotent One, Who rules light
and shade,

Here I am Christ, Thou giver of Life and the Gift of Life itself,
Here I am Christ, all my being sealed unto Thy Will,
Here I am Christ, into Thy service with the strength to save or stay.
Guide and guard Thy servant from all temptation that my honour
may be spotless and my soul remains unstained, Adsum Domine.
Amen.

(Priest rises and uses either a sword or hand casting a ring of Light
clockwise, visualising it passing through all the walls, so that
the entire space is encompassed)

Priest: We stand outside of time, in a place not of this earth, as our
ancestors before us proclaimed: we join together and are one.
By all Thy Holy Angels and all Thy Saints, we call upon Thee,
O Thou Most High, to guard and defend us from all perils:
thus it is, has ever been, and will be for all times to come.
Per omnia Saecula Saeculorum.

All: Amen.

(Priest peforms Asperges the Altar and circle the space with Holy Water)

Priest: In the Name which is above every name and in the Power
of the Father ✠ and of the Son and the Holy Spirit, I exorcise all evil
influences and seeds of evil. I lay upon them the spell of Christ's
Holy Temple, that they may be bound with chains and cast into the
outer darkness, that they trouble not Thy Servants of God.

All: Amen

(Priest incensing the altar and circle the space)

Priest: May Archangel Michael who stands at the right side of the
altar of incense, purify this place. May Holy Michael, Captain of the
Heavenly Hosts and Guardian of the Holy Temple, seal the doors to
the lower realms and bar them with the Burning Sword of Paradise.

All: Amen.

(Priest takes flame from the lit candles upon the altar, light the quarter candles)

Priest: May the Light of Christ, rising in Glory, scatter the darkness, both within and without.

All: In this Light we are protected

Priest: Holy art Thou God, Holy art Thou Mighty One, Holy art Thou Immortal One: pour out Thy Love upon us. Visit, we beseech Thee O Christ, this place and let Thy Holy Angels dwell herein to preserve us in Peace and may Thy Blessing descend upon us forever.

All: Within Thy Blessing we are. Amen.

Quarters

(Making the sign of the Cross in each quarter invoke the four Holy Angels)

East: Holy ✠ Raphael, Healing Hand of God, Guardian of the wind and tempest, may we be guarded and healed in mind and soul.

South: Holy ✠ Michael, Defender and Guardian of the Light and its servants, protect us now and uphold that perfect image of God.

West: Holy ✠ Gabriel, Strength of the Holy One and Heavenly Herald, carry our prayers to our Lady, the Queen of Heaven.

North: Holy ✠ Uriel, Light of the Holy One, Enlighten us and let all ignorance and fear die within this place.

(option: Holy Communion)

Priest (at the altar): O Risen Christ, Immanence of God, Brilliance of the Eternal Light, Who shows us the Way to Truth and Life, O Wisdom and Understanding, Who proceeds from the Mouth of the Most High, reaching from end to end, rigorously and sweetly articulating all, O Cornerstone Who makes the two into one,

O Key of David and Sceptre of the House of Solomon: Come to us.
Illumine us who dwell in darkness and the shadow of death, and lead
us forth from the house of our captivity, transmute the body of
our earthliness, configuring it to the Body of Thy Glory, through
that working whereby Thou art able to subject all to Thyself.

All: Amen.

Priest: Holy Archangel (name Angel of the day) intercede for us....

All: Praise be to (name Angel of the day)

Priest: Our Lady and Queen of Heaven, pray for us. Glory be to the
Father and the Son ✠ and the Holy Spirit, as it was in the beginning,
is now and ever shall be, a world without end.

All: Before you Oh Great Mother, all shadows flee. Amen.

(Any sacrament, ritual or prayer may now be performed)

Closing

Priest: East: Holy Raphael, be Blessed ✠ and return to Thy abode
South: Holy Michael, be Blessed ✠ and return to Thy abode
West: Holy Gabriel, be Blessed ✠ and return to Thy Abode
North: Holy Uriel, be Blessed ✠ and return to Thy Abode
Let all powers drawn by these rites return to their own proper realm
in the power of the Father and the Son ✠ and the Holy Spirit.

All: Amen.

Priest: Unto Thee be the Kingdom, ✠ the Power and the Glory
forever and ever, a world without end.

All: Amen.

Kneeling: saying the Christ's Prayer....

Priest (rising): God, let Thy servant depart in Peace according to Thy Word, for mine eyes have seen Thy Salvation, which Thou has prepared before the face of all people, to be a Light to lighten the gentiles and to be the Glory of Thy people. Glory be to the Father and the Son ✠ and the Holy Spirit.

All: Amen. Unto Thee be the Kingdom, ✠ the Power and the Glory forever and ever, a world without end. Amen.

Priest: The Grace of Christ ✠, the Love of God and the Fellowship of the Holy Spirit, be with us all for evermore.

All: Amen.

Part 3 Celebrations of the year

The Holy Mass of Christmas

A.S.A. APOSTOLIC SUCCESSION OF ARIMATHEA

Opening: stillness, invocation, procession and chant towards the altar

Invocation

Priest - Antiphon: ALLELUIA, ALLELUIA! The Holy One has said, "Thou art My Son, this day I have begotten Thee"

All: A Light shall shine upon us this day, for Christ is born in us

Priest: Unto us a Child is born, unto us a Son is given

All: His Name is called Wonderful Counselor, the Mighty One, the Everlasting Father, and the Prince of Peace

Priest: Of the increase of its rulership and Peace, there shall be no end, to establish the Heavenly Kingdom, for ever and ever

All: Glory be to God in the Highest, and on earth, Peace to those of good will. ALLELUIA, ALLELUIA!

Collect

Priest: Let us pray

All: Almighty and All-Loving God, we celebrate the incarnation of Your Ineffable Light; for by mystery of the Word-made-flesh, Your Glory has shone anew upon our minds, and our hearts are filled with love and joy. We ask Your Grace to be ever mindful of Your Indwelling Presence in the hearts of all humanity; through Christ, Your Immanence within us and all creation. Amen

(Priest performs Asperges, three times self, three times the altar and three times the congregation)

Priest: All Encompassing One, Who ceaselessly creates and sustains,
The fabric of the Universe, send forth Your Holy and Beloved
Angels, To guard, encourage, protect and teach all who dwell within
this place
In Your strength O God, do we command all adverse powers,
to wither into nothingness, that they shall not abide, and that our
temples ☦ within, and our temples ☦ without, may emerge as strong,
pure vessels, to contain the Eternal Mystery, as it unfolds on earth

Congregation: Amen

Lighting of the Four Candles & Invoking the Four Archangels

Priest: I will kindle my fire this Day (Night),
In the Presence of the Four Archangels of Heaven,
In the Presence of Raphael, regent of the Air,
In Presence of Michael, regent of the Fire
In Presence of Gabriel, regent of the Waters
In Presence of Uriel, regent of the Earth,

Without malice, without jealousy,
Without envy, without fear,
Without terror of anyone under the sun

Congregation: God, Kindle Thou in my heart within,
A flame of love to my neighbour,
To my foe, to my friend, to my kindred and all,
To the brave, to the knave, to the thrall,
The Blessings of Heaven be upon us,
From the lowliest creature that liveth,
To the Name that is highest of all,
Amen

Purification & First Censing

Priest: Purify this place O God, and make of us One Body,
Growing into the fullness of Christ,
A Temple of Living Stones, through which Infinite Life may flow,
Let the Angels and Archangels join us in this Work of transforming
the Earth

Addressing penitential rite

Priest: My companions, to prepare ourselves to receive and celebrate
the Sacred Mysteries, let us make our confession before God,
Open yourself before the Mystery and become available to the Source
who has given Its Life for you

Congregation: Create in me a clean heart. O Forgiving Love,
And renew a right Spirit within me,
Here is my body, I cast it down before you,
Heal its imperfections with your perfection and make me whole
Here is my mind, I spread it out before you,
Forgive my foolishness and ignorance with Your Bright Wisdom
Here is my heart, it is Yours alone, forgive its restless wanderings
from You
Here is my life, I offer it unto You, do with me as You will, forgive me,
Together with Yourself, restore unto me, the Joy of Your Salvation,

That I may awake in Your Likeness and be satisfied,
Through Christ, the Indwelling Light,
Amen

Absolution

Priest: The Mercy and Grace of the Son of Light be upon you ☥ will
forgive all your sins and bring us to Eternal Light

Congregation: Amen

KYRIE

All: KYRIE ELEISON
KYRIE ELEISON
KYRIE ELEISON
CHRISTE ELEISON
CHRISTE ELEISON
CHRISTE ELEISON
KYRIE ELEISON
KYRIE ELEISON
KYRIE ELEISON

Gloria

Priest: Glory be to God, the Inmost and Most Highest

Congregation: And Peace to its people on earth. Almighty God our
Father - Mother,
We worship You, we give You thanks, we praise you for your Glory,
Christ, all Redeeming One, Son of the Great Light, Help and Heal us all
You are seated at the Right Hand of the Father, receive our prayer,
For You are the Chief among the Holy Ones, You are the Anointed One,
The Beloved Child, who with the Holy Spirit,
Art one in the ✠ Glory of God
Amen.

Collect

Priest: The Holy One be with you

Congregation: And also with you

Priest: Let us pray

Congregation: O God the Giver of all gifts,
We praise You, the Source of all we have and are
You shelter us beneath the shadow of Your Wings,
And search into the depths of our hearts
Your Light is strong, your Love is here

Remove the blindness that cannot know you, and relieve the fear that
would hide us from Your Sight
Touched by Your hand, our world is Holy,
Open our eyes to see Your Hand at work in the Splendor of Creation,
and the beauty of human life
Draw us beyond the limits, which this world imposes,
To the life where Your Spirit makes all life complete.
We ask this through Your Son the Christ, Your Child,
Who lives and reigns with You and the Holy Spirit,
One God, forever and ever. Amen

Liturgy of the word

Readings

Priest: The first reading is from (appropriate scripture or text follows)

Priest: This is the Word of God, the Logos incarnate

Congregation: Thanks be to God

Gradual

Priest: ALLELUIA, ALLELUIA, With Thee is the Princedom of Thy
Strength, in the Brightness of Thy Saints. From the Womb, before
the day star, I begot Thee.
Glory be to God the Inmost and Most High. Blessed are they that
come in the Name of the Holy One. Sit and rest at my right hand
forever. ALLELUIA, ALLELUIA

Second reading of the Gospel (Priest or altar servant)

Invocation: Cleanse my heart and my lips O Most High, Who by the
Hand of your Angel-Seraph, did cleanse the lips of your Prophets
with that of a burning coal from Your Altar. And in Your loving -
kindness, purify me, that I may proclaim the Holy Gospel
Priest: May the Divine be in your ✠ heart and on your ✠ lips, that
through your heart the Love of God may shine forth and your mouth
may manifest Its Power. Amen

Priest or altar servant: The Holy One be with you

Congregation: And also with you

Priest: This is a reading from the Holy scriptures according to....
(reading)
Priest: This is the Good News according to....

Congregation: Praise to You O Christ

Sermon (meditation)

Credo

Congregation: (spoken)
I Believe in God the Divine Mystery, beyond all definition and all rational understanding, the Heart of all that ever existed, that exists now and ever will exist

I Believe in Christ, Messenger of God's Word, Bringer of Gods Healing, Heart of Gods Compassion, Bright Star in the Firmament, of Gods Prophets, Mystics and Saints

I Believe in the Holy Spirit, the Life of God that is our Innermost Life, the Breath of God moving in our Being, the Depth of God Living in each of us

I Believe that I am called to be Christ's Twin, allowing myself to be a vehicle of God's Love, a Source of Gods Wisdom and Truth, and an instrument of Gods Peace in the World

I Believe that Gods Reign is here and now, stretched out all around us for those with eyes to see it, hearts to receive it and hands to make it happen

I Believe in the community of God seekers, in all religions, the works of the prophets, mystics and saints, and those just beginning their Spiritual Journey

I Believe in a future on this earth, when all will be God-centred and God conscious, when we will learn to live in Peace and Love, in the fellowship of brothers and sisters

I Believe that in death life is changed, not taken away and that we will always go, from step to step in Gods Life, Gods Love and Gods Glory for All Eternity
Amen. Amen. Amen.

Prayers of the Faithful

Priest: My companions, let us call to mind God's many Blessings and ask to hear the prayers which are inspired to ask

Priest: For all of us gathered in this Holy place, in faith, reverence and love of God, that we may offer an acceptable sacrifice
We pray to the Holy One:

Congregation: Beloved One hear our prayer

Priest: For God's Holy Church, within and without and every place of worship at this very moment, and all its devotees and those who lead them. That Christ guide and protect them
We pray to the Holy One:

Congregation: Beloved One hear our prayer

Priest: For all our brothers and sisters in need, that the Holy One guides and assist them all
We pray to the Holy One:

Congregation: Beloved One hear our prayer

Priest: For all the peoples of the world, that God unites them in Peace, Love and Harmony
We pray to the Holy One:

Congregation: Beloved One hear our prayer

Priest: For those who serve us in public office and those entrusted
with the common good
We pray to the Holy One:

Congregation: Beloved One hear our prayer

Priest: For those who are in sickness or in suffering, especially
for those souls who we now name before Thee (read names)
We pray to the Holy One:

Congregation: Beloved One hear our prayer

Priest: For all the departed and those who mourn them. Especially
those who we now name before Thee (read names)
We pray to the Holy One:

Congregation: Beloved One hear our prayer

Priest: And for any special intentions that you may have, said in
silent prayer (pause).... we pray to the Holy One:

Congregation: Beloved One hear our prayer

Priest: Now let us call upon our Heavenly Mother, asking Her to
unite our prayers with Hers, as we say:

Congregation: Hail Mary full of Grace, the Beloved and Holy One is
with Thee. Blessed art Thou amongst women, and Blessed is the
Fruit of thy Womb. Holy Mary, Mother of God, pray for us now,
and at the hour of our victory, over sin, disease and death.
Amen

Sign of Peace

Priest: My companions, we have confessed our sins and we have
been forgiven; Christ the Compassionate King, binds us with a bond
of Love that cannot be broken. Therefore in the Name of the Logos
ever present ever saying: "Peace I leave with you, my Peace I give
unto you; not as the world gives do I give it unto you"

Priest: The Peace of Christ be with you always

Congregation: And also with you

Presentation of the Gifts

(Priest lifts Shroud from the Grail and Paten)

Priest: Leave the mortal and the temporal to the realm of the world, for they are as dust and ash, while I am Immortal and Eternal amongst you. Behold Me as I Am and behold your own face within Me (presentation Shroud)

Priest: Most Holy One, accept that of which by the nature of this planet we are composed, and in our great gratitude, we offer this Bread unto You, as we likewise offer ourselves

Congregation: On this paten O Christ with this Bread, we place all the creative actions of the people of the earth; their aspirations, their joy, their achievements and their work

Priest: Blessed are You, God of all Creation, through Your Goodness we have this Bread to offer, which earth has given and human hands have made It will become for us, our ✠ Bread of Life

Congregation: Blessed be God forever

Priest: As your Spirit would move the heart of every being,
So we move water within this wine, and they shall move as one

Priest: We adore you O God, and offer unto You this water and wine, as we offer that which gives us life. From You have we come and unto You shall we return

Congregation: Into our Chalice with this wine, we pour the sorrows, the pain and the suffering of all your creation. Into this offering of the world, we would gather those closest to us, those whose lives are bound up with our own

Priest: Blessed are You God of all creation, through Your Goodness we have this Wine to offer; fruit of the vine and work of human hands. It will become for us our ✠ Spiritual drink

Congregation: Blessed be God forever

Sign of Bondage

Congregation: With these we unite those more distant and less familiar to us,
The great multitude of humanity, scattered over every part of the globe,

In deepest sympathy and understanding, we unite ourselves,
With the ceaseless pilgrimage of humanity; past, present and future,

With all its joys and sorrows, its hopes and fears, that we may be one with them All

We would draw into this offering every form of life; animals, trees, flowers and fruits, rocks and fire, wind and water, and the very fabric of the earth itself. We offer ourselves, all that we have and all that we are, Let all Existence be now placed on our altar, that we may raise it up to Thee

Second Censing

(Priest performs the censing of the offerings and the congregation)

Priest: receive O Source of Life, this Your manifold Creation, in all its Light and all its Darkness

Congregation: Amen

Lavabo

Priest: I will wash my hands in innocence O God and so I will go to Your Altar and offer your Mystery to those who wish to receive

Orate Fratres

Priest: Pray my companions, that our sacrifice may be acceptable to God

Congregation: May God accept this sacrifice at your hands and sanctify our lives in Its Service

Prayer over the gifts

Priest: May these offerings, Oh Holy One, be as the birth in Bethlehem, and pour Peace upon us. In the same way that Christ, born as a human, also shone as God upon earth, so may this earthly bread and wine mediate to us that which is Divine. Through Christ, the ever reborn Child.

All: Amen

Sursum Corda

Priest: The Holy One be with you
Congregation: And also with you

Priest: Lift up your hearts
Congregation: We lift them up to the Most High

Priest: Let us give thanks to God
Congregation: It is right to give thanks and praise

Preface

Congregation: O Holy One of Blessing, God of all Being
We do well always and everywhere to give You thanks
You have no need of our praise, yet our desire to thank You is itself Your Gift
Our prayer of thanksgiving adds nothing to Your Greatness, but makes us to grow in Your Grace
You give us Your Holy Spirit, the Comforter, to help us always with Her Power, so that with loving trust, we may turn to You in all our troubles and give You thanks in all our joys

Priest: Source of life and goodness, you have created all things,
To fill Your creatures with every Blessing, and lead all to the Joyful
Vision of Your Light. Countless Hosts of Angels, stand before You,
to do Your Will.
They look upon You, and praise You night and day.

United with them, with Angels and Archangels; with Thrones,
Dominations, Princedoms, Virtues and Powers, with Cherubim,
Seraphim and Ashim,
And in the Name of every creature under Heaven,
We too praise Your Glory as we say:

Sanctus

All: Holy! Holy! Holy! God of Power and Might
Heaven and earth are full of Your Glory
Hosanna in the Highest
Blessed are those who come in the Name of the Holy One
Hosanna in the Highest

Canon of the Mass

Priest: Holy One, You are Holy indeed, the Fountain of all Holiness,
As one family we gather around Your Table,
Here is the Sacrifice of Christ offered in Mystery

Here is prepared Christ's Table, at which Your children,
Are nourished by the Body of Christ,
Here Your people drink from the Living Spirit,
The Stream of Living Water, that flows from the Stone of Christ
Loving Creator, we bring You all these gifts of Bread ✠ and Wine ✠
And ourselves as a living sacrifice

Let Your Spirit descend upon these gifts, to make them Holy,
Sanctify them, that they may become,
The Body ✠ and Blood ✠ of Christ,
Who has willed us to make this Eucharist

Consecration

Priest: The Day before He suffered He took Bread into His Sacred Hands,
And with His Eyes lifted up to Heaven, He gave You thanks and praise.
He broke and ✠ blessed the Bread, giving it unto His disciples, saying:

"Take and eat this all of you, for: This is my Body"

Priest: When supper was ended, He took this Cup into His Sacred Hands,
again He gave You thanks and praise. He blessed ✠ the Cup, and
gave it unto His disciples saying:

"Take and drink this all of you, for: This is the Cup of My Blood"

Whenever you do these things I AM is present among you.

Affirmation

All: Thee we adore O Hidden Splendour Thee
Who in Thy Sacrament dost deign to be
We worship Thee beneath this earthly veil
And here Thy Presence we devoutly hail

Priest: Father, we celebrate the Mystery of Christ, we Your people
and your ministers, recall His incarnation and Passion,
His triumphant resurrection from the dead and His ascension into
Your Glory
And from the many gifts You have given us, we offer to You,
God of Glory and Majesty, this Holy and Perfect Sacrifice:
The Bread ✠ of Life
And the Cup of ✠ Eternal Salvation

All: Look with favour on these offerings and accept them as once you
accepted the gifts of Abraham and Sarah, our parents in Faith, and
the Wine and Bread offered by Your High-Priest, Melchizedek.

Priest: Almighty God, we pray that Your Angel may take this Sacrifice
to Your altar on High. There to be offered by those, Who as the Eternal
High Priest, forever offer themselves as the Eternal Sacrifice

And as Christ willed that the Heavenly Sacrifice shall be mirrored
here on earth, so that Your people may be united more closely to You,
We pray for Your servants, Who minister at this altar,
That by celebrating these Mysteries, of the Divine Body ✚ and Blood ✚
They may be filled ✚ with Your Mighty Power and Blessing

Priest: Loving God, we call You Father, but you are the fountain of
Motherhood,
Male and female You created us, in Your own Image and Likeness
May all people come to know, that in You, there is no male or female,
No distinction between race, class or colour, for we are all one within You

All: Through Christ, You give us all these Gifts
You fill them with Life and Goodness
You Bless them and make them Holy

Minor Elevation

Priest: By ✚ Him, with ✚ Him, and in ✚ Him,
In the Unity of the Holy Spirit,
All Glory and Honour is Yours Almighty God
Forever and ever, Amen

Communion Rite & Christ's Prayer

Congregation: Our Father Who art in Heaven, Hallowed be Thy Name,
Thy Kingdom come, Thy Will be done, on earth as it is in Heaven,
Give us this day our daily bread and forgive us our trespasses,
As we forgive those who trespass against us, and lead us not into
temptation, but deliver us from evil
For Thee ✚ is the Kingdom, and the Power and the Glory,
Forever and ever. Amen

Veneration of Saints

Priest: Here we give praise to those channels of Your grace, the Just
Ones made perfect: Enoch, Melchizedek, Yahushua-Christ, Joseph of
Arimathea, Maria Magdalena, John the Beloved, Teresa of Avila,
Jacob Boehme, Meister Eckhart, ... and any other saints or teachers
that you wish to venerate (Silence)....
And we ☩ join with them before Your Great White Throne, from
which flows Infinite Love, Light and Blessing, through all the worlds
that You have made

Fraction

Priest: O Son of God, You show Yourself this day upon countless altars,
Yet, truly remain One and indivisible,
In token of Your great Sacrifice, we break (breaking of the Host) this,
Your Body…
And in token of Your Triumph over ☩ death, and the oneness of Your ☩
Spirit and Body, and Your Glorious ☩ Resurrection, we unite this
Your Body, with this Your Blood (unite)… Praying that by this action
ordained from old, they may be for us, and for all the world,
a channel of Grace and of Life Eternal. Amen

Agnus Dei

Priest: Lamb of God, slain from the Foundation of the world
Congregation: Help and Heal us all

Priest: Lamb of God, slain from the Foundation of the world
Congregation: Help and Heal us all

Priest: Lamb of God, slain from the Foundation of the world
Congregation: Grant us Peace

Priest: This is the Lamb of God slain from the Foundation of
the world, happy are those who take place at His Supper

Congregation: Christ our Passover is sacrificed for us, therefore
let us keep the feast,

As You gave Your Body and Blood, so I offer myself wholly unto You.
My body and my blood, to transform as You Will, that Your Mystery
is completed within me ✠

Communion

(Priest takes and gives out communion)
The Body of Christ ✠ and the Bread of Angels,
The Blood of Christ ✠ and the Grail of Eternal Life

Post communion prayer

Priest: I have eaten Your Sacred Body, no darkness will take me,
I have looked upon it, now my eyes see Your Wonders,
I have not been a stranger to Your Mysteries,
I am never separated from You ✠

Conclusion

Priest: let us pray

Congregation: Under the veil of earthly things, now we are in
communion with the Holy Spirit. With open face we behold Christ,
and being made anew, like unto its own Glorious Body, may we
abide in Your Presence always O God, and serve You night and day.
Amen

Priest: The Mystery is complete and the rite has ended and the
Blessed Archangels depart in Joy and Peace

All: We give thanks to all the Holy Angels of Heaven and to God
Who send them

Priest: The Blessings of God the Creator, the Redeemer ✠ and
the Transforming Spirit. Amen

Priest: Ite Missa Est

Congregation: Deo Gratias

Rite of Candlemas

2nd of February being the Presentation of Christ in the temple
& the purification of the Blessed Lady Mary.

Sanctuary / Temple

No flowers or extra candles on the altar. Just the regular unlit candles.
The candles that are distributed should be on a tray and veiled.
The Monstrance containing the Sanctissisimum, should be in the
vestry, awaiting its procession later in the ceremony. The presiding
minister should also be the celebrant of the Mass, unless a high-priest
or bishop is in attendance who has the right to celebrate.
Otherwise a priest should be appointed for this Mass. High-Priest
or Bishop blesses the candles and will do the pontifical functions like
the Invocation, Absolution, Blessing of incense, the Gospel reading
and the bestowing of the final Benediction.

The Rite

(Celebrant is vested in violet stole and cope, assisting clergy violet
or white only. Clergy enter and Mass begins as usual with
the Invocation, Asperges, Confiteor and Absolution. The lighting
of the candles is omitted here, as it will take place later in the rite.
After the Absolution has been imparted, assistants bring the veiled
tray of candles before the celebrant of the Mass. Taking the
aspergillum the celebrant sprinkles the candles with Holy Water)

Priest: ✠ Our help is in the Name of the Holy One
All: Who has made Heaven and Earth

Priest: O God incline to hear us
All: And let our prayer come to you

Priest: Blessed are those that extend the Light
All: For they shall be called the Servants of God

Priest: Let us Pray

O Christ, Son of the Great Light that indwells the world, grant that
as on this day we receive You with praise in this Your earthly temple,
so may the radiance of Your Compassion shine ever more brightly
within the Temples of our Hearts. Sanctify ♦ these candles and tapers
that, wherever they burn, Your Presence may abide and all evil
be banished thereby. Praise unto you O Christ the Indwelling Light,
before Whose Shining Star of Glory the Angels veil their faces,
praising evermore the Three in One God.

All: Amen

(The candles are now distributed to all assembled in whatever
manner is most appropriate. The clergy now retire. The altar is now
dressed with flowers, many candles and the Monstrance. Clergy in
white vestments. Priest in violet or white. All candles are now lit.
Priest and clergy re-enter the sanctuary and recite the Psalm of Praise
- Benedicite Omnia Opera)

Antiphon: O praise the One al you servants, praise God all nations

Priest: All you works of God of the universe, praise God,
All: Praise the One and magnify Christ forever
Priest: O You Archangels of God,
All: Praise the One and magnify Christ forever
Priest: All Angels of the Light,
All: Praise the One and magnify Christ forever
Priest: O you Heavens,
All: Praise the One and magnify Christ forever
Priest: O you Waters that are above the firmament,
All: Praise the One and magnify Christ forever
Priest: All you Powers-that-be,
All: Praise the One and magnify Christ forever
Priest: O you Sun and Moon,
All: Praise the One and magnify Christ forever
Priest: All you Stars of Heaven,
All: Praise the One and magnify Christ forever
Priest: O you Showers and Rain,
All: Praise the One and magnify Christ forever
Priest: O you Winds of God,

All: Praise the One and magnify Christ forever
Priest: O you Fire and Heat,
All: Praise the One and magnify Christ forever
Priest: O you Winter and Summer,
All: Praise the One and magnify Christ forever
Priest: O you Spring and Autumn,
All: Praise the One and magnify Christ forever
Priest: O you Dews and Rains,
All: Praise the One and magnify Christ forever
Priest: O you frost and Cold,
All: Praise the One and magnify Christ forever
Priest: O you Ice and Snow,
All: Praise the One and magnify Christ forever
Priest: All you Nights and Days,
All: Praise the One and magnify Christ forever
Priest: O you Light and Darkness,
All: Praise the One and magnify Christ forever
Priest: O You Lightning and Clouds,
All: Praise the One and magnify Christ forever
Priest: O the Earth and all its Creatures,
All: Praise the One and magnify Christ forever
Priest: All you Mountains and Hills,
All: Praise the One and magnify Christ forever
Priest: All you Green Plants upon the earth,
All: Praise the One and magnify Christ forever
Priest: All you Lakes and Rivers,
All: Praise the One and magnify Christ forever
Priest: All you Seas and Oceans,
All: Praise the One and magnify Christ forever
Priest: O all that moves within the waters,
All: Praise the One and magnify Christ forever
Priest: O you Birds and all that flies in the air,
All: Praise the One and magnify Christ forever
Priest: All you Creatures and Animals,
All: Praise the One and magnify Christ forever
Priest: All you Hosts of Faery,
All: Praise the One and magnify Christ forever
Priest: All you Children of Adam,
All: Praise the One and magnify Christ forever

Priest: All you Priests and Servants,
All: Praise the One and magnify Christ forever
Priest: All you Teachers and Stewards of the Mysteries,
All: Praise the One and magnify Christ forever
Priest: All you Hierarchs of God,
All: Praise the One and magnify Christ forever
Priest: All you Spirits and Souls of the Righteous,
All: Praise the One and magnify Christ forever
Priest: All you Sacred Humans of Good Heart,
All: Praise the One and magnify Christ forever

Antiphon: O Praise the One all you His servants - praise Christ all you nations.

(Upon reaching the altar the celebrant enthrones the Monstrance, puts incense on the thurible and while all kneeling, incenses the Blessed Sacrament. Then celebrant declares)

Priest: Christ is in the Holy Temple, let all worlds fall silent before Its Presence.

(short period of Silent Adoration)

Priest: Let us pray-
Holy One, make us one with the Angels of Praise in silent prayer, as we joyfully adore Your Majesty, through Christ, the Light of the world.

All: Amen

(Mass now continues with the Lighting of the fires after the Archangelic candles have been lit. All other candles are also lit and Mass continues as usual except that no one's back should be turned towards the Blessed Sacrament. The Sacrament is returned into the Tabernacle after the Holy Communion has been received)

Ash-Wednesday

Invocation

Priest: Help us O most Holy One, to cast from us all iniquity,
that we may enter with pure minds into the Holy of Holies, through
Christ the Master of Love and forgiveness. Amen

All: May the Holy and Righteous Ones, whose pupil we aspire to
become, show us the Light we seek, give us the strong aid of their
compassion and their wisdom,

Priest: There is a Peace that passes understanding, it abides
in the hearts of those who live in the Eternal,
There is a Power that marks all things new, it lives and moves
in those, who know the Self as One,

All: May that Peace brood over us, that power uplift us, till we stand
where the One Initiator is invoked, till we see the Star of Christ
shine forth. Amen

Priest: + In the Name of the Creator, the Redeemer and
the Transforming Spirit. Amen
(Priest gathers the ash from the Mass and / or burns some wood
or paper from the congregation)

All: Let us undo ourselves from the robes of ignorance in which we
have dressed ourselves for ages, hiding from the Light that shines
beyond the fabric of our own mind.

Priest: + (over the olive oil) May this oil be consecrated and become
the Living Substance that rains down from the Highest Heaven,
so it may anoint us like the Dew of Christ, and may it bestow upon us
the Light of the Immanent Presence that will prepare us for this
period of inner stillness and peace.
All: Amen

Priest: + (over the ash before you) These ashes are the remains
of the Holy Fire which transforms all things and all creatures into
the likeness of God. These are the Holy remnants of the Fire of Christ
that washes all clean and makes all pure. They remind us of our inner
life that is directed towards our physical temple within, which carries
for the time it endures on earth, the Fire and Light of God.

(Priest dips right index finger into the Oil and then into the Ash
and makes a cross on his / her forehead 3 times....)

Priest: "EMPHATA - I open myself"

(In this way the priest crosses all those who come to the altar
and wish to receive)

All: Emphata. Amen.

Holy Communion

(end of the rite)

The Third Eye (Daath) is opened as an entrance of new inspiration
and life. The Vision of Unity is invited to become yours.

Now, we start the period of Lent, a fasting period of meats, alcohol
and other stimulating substances. It is also a psychological fasting
of personal thoughts and feelings. Abstain from impure thoughts,
ideas and memories. Write these down on paper so you may burn
these later. Observe your actions and "fast" within the world of
action, abstaining from impure actions. Keep reminding to open
yourself to the Higher worlds of Briah and Aziluth.

Maundy Thursday or White Thursday

In the A.S.A. we celebrate white Thursday with a short version
of the Mass or Communion. Prior to the celebration Holy water
is consecrated and Holy oil for the cycle of Easter.

Many candles are lit, flowers adorn the altar and the sacrament
is present on the altar in the monstrance and veiled in white.
The celebration is in the evening time. Monstrance is unveiled after
the ablutions. Two hosts are consecrated: one for the celebration
and one to be placed in the Tabernacle (used for Eastern day).
Altar cloth is white.

Preparations

After the service: ciborium with host and monstrance carrying
the host are locked away. The altar is stripped and candles are
extinguished. Altar is dressed in violet or dark colour.

Washing of feet: takes place after the sign of peace in the Eucharist.

Maundy Thursday is the Thursday before Easter, believed to be
the day when Jesus celebrated his final Passover with His disciples.
Most notably, that Passover meal where Jesus washed the feet of
his disciples in an extraordinary display of humility.
He then commanded them to do the same for each other.

Humbleness is one of the virtues on this day of consecration.
Christ's "mandate" is commemorated on Maundy Thursday.
"Maundy" being a shortened form of mandatum (Latin), which means
"command." It was on the Thursday of Christ's final week before
being crucified and resurrected that He gave this commandment to
His disciples. Jesus and his disciples had just shared what was known
as the Last Supper and he was washing their feet when he stated:

"A new commandment I give to you, that you love one another: just as I have loved you, you also are to love one another" (John 13:34)
What was the New Commandment?
This is the Commandment of Love. Jesus sacrificially met his followers' deepest need; a new spiritual life and the forgiveness of sins. He even loved His enemies, and he calls us to show love to those who don't appear to deserve it. Just as Jesus loved sinners "to the end" (John 13:1) when he had nothing to gain from them, so must we. The Bible says that there was nothing attractive about sinful mankind that drew Him to love us. God loved us while we were yet sinners (Romans 5:8). Salvation is not only a wonderful gift that protects us from the penalty that we deserve (Romans 6:23) but the work of Christ also imbues new life, grants spiritual strength, and motivates Divine action in those who believe.
Love is the second virtue on this day where we are invited to behold the whole of humanity as a family and all creatures and beings as one Forgiveness is not synonym but rises forth out of love and is the third virtue on this day.
"Beloved, let us love one another. For love is from God, and whoever loves has been born of God and knows God. Anyone who does not love does not know God, because God is love" (1 John 4:7-8)
Service is the fourth and final virtue on Maundy Thursday.

Maundy Thursday Bible Verses

Luke 22:27-38 - " When the hour came, Yahushua and his apostles reclined at the table. And he said to them, "I have eagerly desired to eat this Passover with you before I suffer. For I tell you, I will not eat it again until it finds fulfilment in the Kingdom of God." After taking the cup, he gave thanks and said, "Take this and divide it among you. For I tell you I will not drink again from the fruit of the vine until the kingdom of God comes." And he took bread, gave thanks and broke it, and gave it to them, saying, "This is my body given for you - do this in remembrance of me".

John 13:2-17 - "Yahushua knew that the Father had put all things under his power, and that he had come from God and was returning to God, so he got up from the meal, took off his outer clothing, and wrapped a towel around his waist.

After that, he poured water into a basin and began to wash his disciples' feet, drying them with the towel that was wrapped around him. He came to Simon Peter, who said to him, "Christ, are you going to wash my feet?" Yahushua replied, "You do not realize now what I am doing, but later you will understand." "No," said Peter, "you shall never wash my feet." Yahushua answered, "Unless I wash you, you have no part with me." "Then, Christ," Simon Peter replied, "not just my feet but my hands and my head as well".

Philippians 2:1-11 - "Therefore if you have any encouragement from being united with Christ, if any comfort from his love, if any common sharing in the Spirit, if any tenderness and compassion, then make my joy complete by being like-minded, having the same love, being one in spirit and of one mind. Do nothing out of selfish ambition or vain conceit. Rather, in humility value others above yourselves, not looking to your own interests but each of you to the interests of the others. In your relationships with one another, have the same mind-set as those who, being in very nature like God, did not consider equality with God something to be used to his own advantage. Rather, he made himself nothing by taking the very nature of a servant, being made in human likeness".

The Holy Mass (shorter form) Maundy Thursday

Priest enters and stands before the altar. A moment of silence…

Priest: In the Name of God, the Creator, the + Redeemer and the Transforming Spirit

All: Amen

(Priest performs Aspergil - three times Himself, three times the altar and three times the congregation)

Priest: All Encompassing One, Who ceaselessly creates and sustains, The fabric of the Universe, send forth Your Holy and beloved Angels, To guard, encourage, protect and teach all who dwell within this place. In Your strength O God, do we command all adverse powers, to wither into nothingness, that they shall not abide, And that our temples + within, and our temples + without, May emerge as strong, pure vessels, To contain the Eternal Mystery, as it unfolds on earth

Lighting of the Four candles

Priest: I will kindle my fire this night, In the Presence of the four Archangels of Heaven; In the Presence of Raphael, regent of the Air, In Presence of Michael, regent of the Fire In Presence of Gabriel, regent of the Waters In Presence of Uriel, regent of the Earth,

Without malice, without jealousy, Without envy, without fear, Without terror of anyone under the sun

All: God, Kindle Thou in my heart within,
A flame of love to my neighbour,
To my foe, to my friend, to my kindred and all,
To the brave, to the knave, to the thrall,
The Blessings of Heaven be upon us,
From the lowliest creature that lives,
To the Name that is Highest of all,
Amen

Purification

(First censing, invocation of the Angel of Christ)

Priest: Purify this place O God, and make of us One Body, Growing into the Fullness of Christ, a Temple of Living Stones, through which Infinite Life may flow,
Let the Angels and Archangels join us in this Work of transforming the Earth

Addressing Penitential Rite

Priest: My companions, to prepare ourselves to receive and celebrate the Sacred Mysteries, let us make our confessions to God

All: Create in me a clean heart. O forgiving Love,
And renew a right Spirit within me
Here is my body, I cast it down before you,
Heal its imperfections with your perfection and make me whole.
Here is my mind, I spread it out before you,
Forgive my foolishness and ignorance with Your bright wisdom.

Here is my heart, it is Yours alone,
Forgive its restless wanderings from You.
Here is my life, I offer it unto You,
Do with me as You will, forgive me,
Together with yourself, restore unto me, the joy of Your Salvation,
That I may awake in Your likeness and be satisfied,
Through Christ, the Indwelling Light,
Amen

Absolution

Priest: The Mercy and Grace of God be upon you + will forgive all sins and bring us to Eternal Light

All: Amen

Collect

Priest: Christ the Immanent Light be with you

All: And also with you

Priest: Let us pray

All: O God the Giver of all gifts,
We praise You, the Source of all we have and are,
You shelter us beneath the shadow of Your Wings,
And search into the debts of our hearts.
Your Light is strong, your Love is here.
Remove the blindness that cannot know you, and relieve the fear that would hide us from Your Sight.
Touched by Your hand, our world is Holy,
Open our eyes to see Your hand at work in the splendor of creation, and the beauty of human life.

Draw us beyond the limits, which this world imposes,
To the life where Your Spirit makes all life complete.
We ask this through Your Son the Christ, your Child,
Who lives and reigns with You and the Holy Spirit,
One God, forever and ever
Amen

Readings from Philippians, Luke and John

Priest: These are the three spiritual virtues of the Last Supper:
Love, Forgiveness and Humbleness

Sign of Peace

Priest: My companions, we have confessed our sins and we have
been forgiven; Christ the Compassionate King, binds us with a bond
of Love that cannot be broken. Therefore in the Name of the Logos
ever present ever saying: "Peace I leave with you, my Peace I give
unto you, not as the world gives do I give it unto you"

The Peace and the Love of Christ be always with you

Congregation: And also with you
(exchange sign of Peace)

Washing of feet - saying: "This is the new Maundatum - a new
commandment I give you, that you love one another, just as I love
you, that you love those close to you and your enemies alike"

All: From this day forward I will follow in your humbleness
and lovingkindness

Presentation of the Gifts

(Priest raises paten)

Priest: Most Holy One, accept that of which by the nature of this
planet we are composed, and in our great gratitude, we offer this
Bread unto You, as we likewise offer ourselves.

All: On this paten O Christ, with this Bread, we place all the creative
actions of the peoples of the earth, their aspirations, their joy,
their achievements and their work.

Priest: Blessed are You, God of all creation. Through Your Goodness
we have this bread to offer, which earth has given and human hands
have made.
It will become for us, our + Bread of Life.

All: Blessed be God forever

(Priest fills the Cup)

As your Spirit would move the heart of every being,
Now we move water within this wine, and they shall move as one.

Priest: We adore you O God, and offer unto You this Water and
Wine, as we offer that which gives us life. From You have we come
and unto You shall we return.

All: Into our Chalice with this wine, we pour the sorrows, the pain
and the suffering of all your creation. Into this offering of the world,
we would gather, those closest to us, those whose lives are bound up
with our own.

Priest: Blessed are You God of all creation, through Your Goodness
we have this wine to offer; fruit of the vine and work of human
hands.
It will become for us our + Spiritual Drink

All: Blessed be God forever

Prayer over the gifts

Priest: Most Holy One, by these Holy Gifts we offer, make + Holy
those who gather in Your Name. May we share this sacrament and
experience the life and power it promises and enter your Presence.
Amen

Sursum Corda

Priest: Christ be with you
Congregation: And also with you

Priest: Lift up your hearts
Congregation: We lift them up to the Most High

Priest: Let us give thanks to the One-Who-is Openness
Congregation: It is right to give thanks and praise

Preface

Priest: O Holy One of Blessing, God of all Being
We do well always and everywhere to give You thanks.
You have no need of our praise, yet our desire to thank You is itself
Your Gift. Our prayer of thanksgiving adds nothing to Your Greatness,
but makes us to grow in Your Grace.
You give us Your Holy Spirit, the Comforter, to help us always with
Her Power; so that with loving trust, we may turn to You in all our
troubles and give You thanks in all our joys

Source of Life and Goodness; You have created all things,
To fill Your creatures with every Blessing, and lead all to the joyful
vision of Your Light.

Countless Hosts of Angels, stand before You, to do Your Will.
They look upon You, and praise you night and day.
United with them; with Angels and Archangels; with Thrones,
dominations, Princedoms, Virtues and Powers,
With Cherubim, Seraphim and Ashim,
And in the name of every creature under Heaven,
We too praise Your Glory as we say:

Sanctus

ALL: Holy! Holy! Holy! God of Power and Might
Heaven and earth are full of Your Glory
Hosanna in the Highest.
Blessed are they who come in the Name of Christ
Hosanna in the Highest

Canon of the mass

Priest: You are Holy indeed; the Fountain of all Holiness,
As one family we gather around Your Table,
Here is the Sacrifice of Christ offered in mystery

Here is prepared Christ's Table, at which Your children,
Are nourished by the Body of Christ,

Here Your people drink from the Living Spirit,
The stream of Living Water, that flows from the Stone of Christ.
Loving Creator, we bring You all these Gifts of Bread + and Wine +
And ourselves as a Living Sacrifice

Let Your Spirit descend upon these Gifts, to make them Holy;
Sanctify them, that they may become;
The Body + and Blood + of Christ,
Who has willed us to make this Eucharist

Consecration

Priest: The day before He suffered He took Bread into His Sacred Hands,
And with His eyes lifted up to Heaven, He gave You thanks and praise.
He broke and + blessed the Bread, giving it unto His disciples, saying:

"Take and eat this all of you, for
This is My Body"

When supper was ended, He took this Cup into His Sacred Hands,
Again He gave You thanks and praise. He blessed + the Cup, and
gave it unto His disciples saying:

"Take and drink this all of you, for:
This is the Cup of My Blood"

Whenever you do these things I AM is present among you!

Affirmation

All: Thee we adore O Hidden Splendour Thee
Who in Thy sacrament dost deign to be
We worship Thee beneath this earthly veil
And here Thy Presence we devoutly hail

Priest: Almighty God, we pray that Your Angel may take this sacrifice
to Your altar on High. There to be offered by them, Who as the Eternal
High Priest, forever offer themselves as the Eternal Sacrifice

And as Christ has willed that the Heavenly Sacrifice shall be
mirrored here on earth, so that Your people may be united more
closely to You.
We pray for Your servants, Who minister at this altar,
That by celebrating these mysteries, of the Divine Body + and Blood
+ They may be filled + with Your Mighty Power and Blessing

Minor Elevation

Priest: By + Him, with + Him and in + Him,
In the unity of the Holy Spirit,
All Glory and Honour is Yours Almighty God
Forever and ever

All: Amen

Communion rite

Fraction

Priest: O Son of God, You show Yourself this day upon countless altars,
Yet, truly remain One and Indivisible.
In token of Your Great Sacrifice, we break (breaking of the Hosts) this,
Your Body. And in token of Your Triumph over + death, and
the Oneness of
Your + Spirit and Body, and Your Glorious + Resurrection, we unite
this Your Body, with this Your Blood (unite). Praying that by this
action, ordained from old, they may be for us, and for all the world,
a channel of Grace and of Life Eternal.

All: Amen

(Priest gives out communion)

"The Body of Christ + and the Bread of Angels,
The Blood of Christ + and the Grail of Eternal Life"

Ablutions & Post communion prayer

Priest: I have eaten Your sacred Body, no darkness will take me,
I have looked upon it, now my eyes see Your Wonders,
I have not been a stranger to Your Mysteries,
I am never separated from You ☦

Conclusion

Priest: The Blessing of God the Creator, the Redeemer + and
the Transforming Spirit.

All: Amen

Priest: The ritual of Christ will now be closed and the blessed
Archangels and Angels return to their abode in Peace

All: We give thanks to all the Hierarchies of Heaven and to God
Who send them. Amen

Priest: Ite Missa est

All: Deo Gratias

Good Friday

Traditionally three possible services may be held:
- Prime (morning)
- Veneration of the Cross
- Compline (evening)

No candles are lighted and no incense is used. Altar is left unadorned
except for violet or dark coloured cloth. All crosses are veiled.
This Eucharist service may be done in a whispered tone and eyes
mostly directed towards the earth.
Holy Communion rite is performed in soft spoken way (no singing)
or communion in silence

Administration of the Holy Communion
(According the usage of the A.S.A. Apostolic Succession of Arimathea)

Invocation

Priest: In the Name of God, the Creator ✝, the Redeemer and
the Transforming Spirit.

All: Amen

Priest: My brothers and sisters, companions and fellow-travellers
of The Way, to prepare ourselves to receive the Sacred Mysteries,
let us make our confession before God.

All: Create in me a clean heart O forgiving Love,
And renew a right Spirit within me,
Here is my body, I cast it down before You,
Heal its imperfections with Your perfection and make me whole.
Here is my mind, I spread it out before You,
Forgive my foolishness and ignorance with Your Bright Wisdom.
Here is my heart, it is Yours alone,
Forgive its restless wanderings from You.

Here is my life, I offer it unto You,
Do with me as You will, forgive me,
Together with Yourself, restore unto me, the Joy of Your Salvation,
That I may awake in Your likeness and be satisfied,
Through Christ, the Indwelling Light,
Amen

Absolution

Priest: The Mercy and Grace of God be upon you ✠ and will liberate you from all sins and bring us to Eternal Light

Priest: let us pray with confidence to the Father, the One-Who-is-Openness in the words that Christ taught us

Prayer

All: Our Father Who art in Heaven, Hallowed be Thy Name,
Thy Kingdom come, Thy Will be done,
On earth as it is in Heaven,
Give us this day our daily bread and forgive us our trespasses,
As we forgive those who trespass against us,
And lead us not into temptation, but deliver us from evil,
For Thine is the Kingdom ✠ and the Power and the Glory,
Forever and ever. Amen

Opening of the Tabernacle

Priest: O God the Life of worlds in this wonderful Sacrament of the altar, You have given us a living memorial of Your endless Love for humanity. As we partake of this Sacred Mystery of Your Body and Blood, draw us now into Mystic Communion with You,

May our souls rise into the immensity of Your Love and may we perceive within ourselves Your abiding Presence, and may we come to know that through You we are also one with all that lives. O Thou the Giver of the Manna of Heaven, who lives and reigns in the hearts of all.

All: Amen

Priest: This is the Lamb of God Slain ✟ from the Foundation of the World, happy are those who partake of Christ's Supper

Communion

Priest: The Body of Christ and the Bread of Angels

Communicant: Amen

Meditation

"And after the Holy Communion they sat in a circle, where Yahushua occupied the centre, and soon they were visited by Roman soldiers accompanied with priests from the Sanhedrin. Accused of falsehood and blasphemy, Yahushua was arrested and taken like a criminal. Almost all disciples stayed there and then, mesmerized, shocked, grieved, afraid and terrified. Why would the Master follow so peacefully the accusers who imprison or even execute him?

The peace was least understood by Peter who took one of the swords of a soldier and cut of an ear. Yahushua corrected Peter, asking him why he would do such a thing after all he taught him. Peter had to give back the sword and sow the ear of the soldier back on. Yahushua was brought before a council of the Sanhedrin which asked for the judgement of Pontius Pilatus, the governing Roman of Judea at the time. He wished order and social structure and was not interested in religious disputes. Pilate was only concerned with the rumours saying that Yahushua was the king of the Jews. Yahushua said to give unto Cesar what belongs to Cesar.
"My Kingdom is not of the earth and will not come by expectations, He said"....

Regardless, the people and priests asked for a crucifixion together with the two criminals standing at either side of the Master. A political and ideological decision had to be made. Pilate asked the priests to decide in order that he could wash his hands in innocence.
The priests of the Sanhedrin did not believe Yahushua being a Messiah. Sadly, He himself never said he was the Messiah, nor that he was a king.... But spoke only about how to enter the Kingdom of God.

The judgement was made and the crucifixion prepared. For those who could bear and witness the ritual of death, some followed up the hill of Golgotha or the hill of skulls.

Yahushua carries his cross up the hill while you and other disciples follow. The sky overhead is clear blue and the hot sun is shining. You can smell a mixture of fear and hate in the air while some people are against the persecuted messiah and others watch in horror when the morbid procession continues.

You have a choice and may be persecuted like Yahushua if soldiers or lay-people find out about your sympathies. A choice that will testify if you will follow your heart or the opinions and judgements of the world.... Where lies your devotion? Are you reliable towards the Teachings of Christ?

If you proceed up the hill of the dead, you will bear your own cross. Dragging your own cross means you will take up the sins of yourself and of others who cannot forgive themselves. The cross is also the symbol of your spiritual responsibility and your willingness to sacrifice yourself in order to become God. If you follow in the footsteps of Christ, this suffering will lead to salvation and liberation. Liberation of what? Liberation from yourself!

At the top of the hill the three men are taken up the large wooden crosses. They are fixated by nails and ropes. The two men at the side of Yahushua moan in agony and ask for mercy. They do not know their immortal self and are terrified of death. They do not see, like most people, that this is the Hill of Transformation. Soon they are hanging on their cross and a slow death sets in. Yahushua does not seem to be occupied with the suffering only, but speaks to Heaven as he looks up, asking his Father to forgive these people for they do not know what they are doing. Forgiveness of those that oppose you or even wish you evil and kill you. One of the man next to him asks to take him to Heaven.... Yahushua answers that he should not be afraid and be assured that he will find his place in Heaven next to him. Then, Yahushua says that it is finished.... breathing out his last breath....

The walls of the Temple crack and the veil between the great hall
and the holy of holies is torn apart.
Slowly the people disappear from the hill and the Romans take down
the dead bodies. Before they throw away the three into a dead pit,
a man comes rushing up the hill. He is a member of the Sanhedrin
and has a document declaring that he is allowed by Pontius Pilate
to confiscate the body of Yahushua to lay him down in his private,
family tomb. The man is called Joseph of Arimathea.

The request is honoured and you and Arimathea together with
other disciples collect the corpse of Yahushua to bring him into
the Sepulchre of Arimathea.

There you enter and prepare the body for the Tomb. All pray for
Yahushua to enter the realm of God and that they may witness his
promise: that he will rise within three days and be with them again.
All lights are extinguished and we remain in stillness in the Presence
of Him.... than, Joseph lights a single candle, sitting at the head of
Yahushua and we all stand next to the body for the last time.
You look into the Face of Yahushua and see a Divine Radiance and
in His Face you see your own face like looking into a pool of water
during a summers day....
In this way you leave the tomb of Arimathea."

Priest: let us pray

Priest: Under the Veil of earthly things now have we communion
with the Christ, soon with open face shall we see Him, and being
made anew like unto His own Glorious Body, may we come before
Your Presence and serve You night and day. Amen

All: Most Holy One, now let Thy servant depart in Peace according
to Thy Word,
For mine eyes have seen Thy Salvation which Thou has prepared
before the face of all people, to be Light to Lighten the gentiles and
to be the Glory of Thy people within the Kingdom of Heaven.

Priest: Unto God's Gracious Love and Protection we commit you.
Christ Bless ✠ and keep you,
The Anointed makes Its Face to shine upon you and be Gracious unto you,
Christ lifts up the Light of Its Countenance upon you and give
Its Peace, now and forever more

All: Amen

(all depart in silence or remain in meditation)

Holy Saturday

A.S.A. APOSTOLIC SUCCESSION OF ARIMATHEA

Rite of the Vigil of Easter

Time: sunset local time
Vestments: white or gold
Outside the temple: the Paschal Candle (unlit), a vessel holding
the Sacred fire kindled. Sacred oil. The Blessed Sacrament in a veiled
Monstrance. A bell is present.
In the sanctuary: unlit candles upon the altar, flowers before Paschal
candle holder. Requirements for a Baptism, Confirmation or / and
Solemn Benediction. Two lights of the Good Friday service are
burning. People receive a little candle (unlit)

The Rite

Priest: In the Name of God, the Creator, the Redeemer
and the Transforming Spirit ✠

All: Amen

Aspergillum with Holy Water

Priest: All Encompassing One, Who ceaselessly creates and sustains,
The fabric of the Universe, send forth Your Holy and Beloved Angels,
To guard, encourage, protect and teach all who dwell within this place
In Your strength Oh God, do we command all adverse powers,
to wither into nothingness, that they shall not abide,
And that our temples + within, and our temples + without,
May emerge as strong, pure vessels,
To contain the Eternal Mystery, as it unfolds on earth

All: Amen

(All now process in silence to the outside. All lights are still
extinguished inside the temple)

(Priest blesses the fire)
Priest: Let this fire, kindled in memory of the Risen Christ
be Purified ✠ and Blessed ✠ by the One who is the never-setting
Sun of Righteousness

All: Amen

(Priest blesses the Paschal candle with oil)
Priest: Let this candle, symbol of the Glorious Resurrection Body,
be Purified ✠ and Blessed ✠ by the One Who is the Light of the world

All: Amen

(Priest lights Paschal candle)
Priest: May the Light of Christ, the Rising Glory, scatter the darkness,
both within and without

All: Amen

(All return into the temple. Priest carries Paschal candle and
genuflects four times when approaching the altar intoning)

Priest: The Light of Christ

All: May this Light shine from our hearts

(Having reached the altar, the priest places the Paschal candle in its
holder. Priest or Deacon comes to the altar and prays)

Priest: Cleanse my heart and my lips O God, who by the hand of
your Angel-Seraph did cleanse the lips of the prophet Isaiah with
a burning coal from Your altar, and in Your Lovingkindness,
purify me that I may be worthy and proclaim the Holy Gospel

Priest: May the Holy One be in your heart ✠ and on your lips ✠-
that through your heart the Love of God may shine forth and through
your lips Its Power may be manifested.

All: Amen.

Reading of the Gospel in front of the Paschal candle

Priest: Christ be with you

All: And also with you

Priest: A reading from the Gospel of Matthew

All: Glory be to you O most Holy One

Matthew:
"When the evening had come, there came a rich man of Arimathea,
named Joseph, who was also a disciple of Yahushua. He went to
Pilate and begged for the body of Yahushua. Then Pilate commanded
for the body to be delivered. And when Joseph had taken the body,
he wrapped it in a clean linen cloth and laid it in his own tomb,
which he had hewn out of a rock. He rolled a great stone before
the sepulchre and departed. And there came Mary Magdalene
and Mary his mother sitting by the Sepulchre.

Now the next day that followed which was the day of preparation,
the chief priests and Pharisees came together unto Pilate saying:

"Sir, we remember that the deceiver said while he was alive, that
he would rise again after three days… he would destroy the temple
and rebuilt it in three days. Command therefore that the Sepulchre
be made sure until the third day and that his disciples will not come
and steal his body. For then they will say that he had risen from
the dead". Pilate said unto them: "See for yourself and be on your
way and convince yourself"

So they went and made the Sepulchre sure, sealing the stone
and setting a watch"

Priest: This is the Gospel according to Matthew

All: Praise be to you O Christ

(Priest affixes the five grains of incense into the Paschal candle)
Priest: Christ yesterday and today - the beginning and the end - Alpha and Omega. Christ is the seasons and the ages. Christ reigns in Glory and Dominion through all the ages of Eternity.

All: Amen.

(Priest purifies Paschal candle with incense and the other candles are lit with the Paschal candle)

Priest: The Divine Fire is kindled on this most Holy night, in presence of the Holy Angels of Heaven:

In presence of Raphael regent of Air,
In presence of Michael regent of Fire,
In presence of Gabriel regent of Water,
In presence of Uriel regent of Earth,

The Blessing of Heaven ✠ be upon us from the lowliest creature that lives, to the Name that is Highest of All.

All: Amen

(The candles held by all present are lit, then the priest proclaims)

Priest: Let the Angelic Choirs of Heaven now rejoice; let the Divine Mysteries be joyfully celebrated and the sacred trumpet resound for the victory of so great a King! Let the whole world also rejoice, illuminated with such resplendent Glory, and let the darkness of the world be dispelled. Let all our temples and places of sacred worship rejoice, adorned with the rays of the Son of Light, and may this temple resound with the joyful voices of all people.

All: Amen.

Priest: Let us pray (invite all)

Priest: O Father of Light in whom is no darkness at all; we praise
and thank You for this most Holy Mystery of the Resurrection.
For in it is prefigured the time when we too shall be raised in Glory
and serve you, clad in deathless bodies of rainbow light. As at this
time, the Christ-Light descended from the tomb to harrow hell,
freeing those trapped in the dark dimensions of their soul.
We pray for your Perpetual Light to liberate all purged souls and
fashion for them a gently shining path unto Paradise. And we also
pray that the Light of the resurrection may redeem the nations,
dissolve the chains of fear, ignorance and hate and bring all children
of mankind - of Adam and Eve - into Your Tabernacle.

May the effulgent Temple of Peace, wherein Your Presence shines
manifest upon earth and Bless all beings. We ask this through Christ,
the Risen One, Who is One with You, in the union of the Holy Spirit,
forever and ever.

All: Amen

(If a Baptism follows the base of the Paschal candle is lowered into
the vessel of Holy water making with it the sign of the cross thrice)

Priest: In the Name of the Father ✝ and the Son ✝ and the Holy Spirit ✝.

All: Amen

(All retire to bring the Sacrament in the Monstrance with
the Omnia Opera)

Antiphon: - O praise the One al you servants - praise God all nations

Priest: All you works of God of the universe, praise God,
All: Praise the One and magnify God forever
Priest: O You Archangels of God,
All: Praise the One and magnify God forever
Priest: All Angels of the Light,
All: Praise the One and magnify God forever

Priest: O you Heavens,
All: Praise the One and magnify God forever
Priest: O you Waters that are above the firmament,
All: Praise the One and magnify God forever
Priest: All you Powers-that-be,
All: Praise the One and magnify God forever
Priest: O you Sun and Moon,
All: Praise the One and magnify God forever
Priest: All you Stars of Heaven,
All: Praise the One and magnify God forever
Priest: O you Showers and Rain,
All: Praise the One and magnify God forever
Priest: O you Winds of God,
All: Praise the One and magnify God forever
Priest: O you Fire and Heat,
All: Praise the One and magnify God forever
Priest: O you Winter and Summer,
All: Praise the One and magnify God forever
Priest: O you Spring and Autumn,
All: Praise the One and magnify God forever
Priest: O you Dews and Rains,
All: Praise the One and magnify God forever
Priest: O you frost and Cold,
All: Praise the One and magnify God forever
Priest: O you Ice and Snow,
All: Praise the One and magnify God forever
Priest: All you Nights and Days,
All: Praise the One and magnify God forever
Priest: O you Light and Darkness,
All: Praise the One and magnify God forever
Priest: O You Lightning and Clouds,
All: Praise the One and magnify God forever
Priest: O the Earth and all its Creatures,
All: Praise the One and magnify God forever
Priest: All you Mountains and Hills,
All: Praise the One and magnify God forever
Priest: All you Green Plants upon the earth,
All: Praise the One and magnify God forever

Priest: All you Lakes and Rivers,
All: Praise the One and magnify God forever
Priest: All you Seas and Oceans,
All: Praise the One and magnify God forever
Priest: O all that moves within the waters,
All: Praise the One and magnify God forever
Priest: O you Birds and all that flies in the air,
All: Praise the One and magnify God forever
Priest: All you Creatures and Animals,
All: Praise the One and magnify God forever
Priest: All you Hosts of Faery,
All: Praise the One and magnify God forever
Priest: All you Children of Adam,
All: Praise the One and magnify God forever
Priest: All you Priests and Servants,
All: Praise the One and magnify God forever
Priest: All you Teachers and Stewards of the Mysteries,
All: Praise the One and magnify God forever
Priest: All you Hierarchs of God,
All: Praise the One and magnify God forever
Priest: All you Spirits and Souls of the Righteous,
All: Praise the One and magnify God forever
Priest: All you Sacred Humans of Good Heart,
All: Praise the One and magnify God forever

Antiphon: O Praise the One all you servants - praise God all you nations.

(The Rite of Solemn Benediction follows in the usual manner.
After the Rite, Easter Vigil may be undertaken by the Clergy and
Servants. Paschal Candle is lit during all ceremonies throughout
the 40 days between Easter and Ascension Day)

Benedicta Omnia Opera

Antiphon: - O praise the One al you servants - praise God all nations

Priest: All you works of God of the universe, praise God,
All: Praise the One and magnify God forever
Priest: O You Archangels of God,
All: Praise the One and magnify God forever
Priest: All Angels of the Light,
All: Praise the One and magnify God forever
Priest: O you Heavens,
All: Praise the One and magnify God forever
Priest: O you Waters that are above the firmament,
All: Praise the One and magnify God forever
Priest: All you Powers-that-be,
All: Praise the One and magnify God forever
Priest: O you Sun and Moon,
All: Praise the One and magnify God forever
Priest: All you Stars of Heaven,
All: Praise the One and magnify God forever
Priest: O you Showers and Rain,
All: Praise the One and magnify God forever
Priest: O you Winds of God,
All: Praise the One and magnify God forever
Priest: O you Fire and Heat,
All: Praise the One and magnify God forever
Priest: O you Winter and Summer,
All: Praise the One and magnify God forever
Priest: O you Spring and Autumn,
All: Praise the One and magnify God forever
Priest: O you Dews and Rains,
All: Praise the One and magnify God forever
Priest: O you frost and Cold,
All: Praise the One and magnify God forever
Priest: O you Ice and Snow,
All: Praise the One and magnify God forever

Priest: All you Nights and Days,
All: Praise the One and magnify God forever
Priest: O you Light and Darkness,
All: Praise the One and magnify God forever
Priest: O You Lightning and Clouds,
All: Praise the One and magnify God forever
Priest: O the Earth and all its Creatures,
All: Praise the One and magnify God forever
Priest: All you Mountains and Hills,
All: Praise the One and magnify God forever
Priest: All you Green Plants upon the earth,
All: Praise the One and magnify God forever
Priest: All you Lakes and Rivers,
All: Praise the One and magnify God forever
Priest: All you Seas and Oceans,
All: Praise the One and magnify God forever
Priest: O all that moves within the waters,
All: Praise the One and magnify God forever
Priest: O you Birds and all that flies in the air,
All: Praise the One and magnify God forever
Priest: All you Creatures and Animals,
All: Praise the One and magnify God forever
Priest: All you Hosts of Faery,
All: Praise the One and magnify God forever
Priest: All you Children of Adam,
All: Praise the One and magnify God forever
Priest: All you Priests and Servants,
All: Praise the One and magnify God forever
Priest: All you Teachers and Stewards of the Mysteries,
All: Praise the One and magnify God forever
Priest: All you Hierarchs of God,
All: Praise the One and magnify God forever
Priest: All you Spirits and Souls of the Righteous,
All: Praise the One and magnify God forever
Priest: All you Sacred Humans of Good Heart,
All: Praise the One and magnify God forever

Antiphon: O Praise the One all you servants - praise God all you nations

Solemn Benediction
of the Blessed Sacrament

A.S.A. APOSTOLIC SUCCESSION OF ARIMATHEA

Having reached the altar the priest invokes

Priest: In the Name of God the Creator, the Redeemer ✠ and
the Transforming Spirit

All: Amen

(All remain while priest goes to the altar to unveil the Monstrance.
The Sacrament incense thrice. Priest says / sings)

O Salutaris Hostia
O Saving Victor, opening wide, The gate of Heaven to us below,
Our foes press in from every side, Thine aid supply, Thy strength bestow,
All praise and thanks to Thee ascend, forevermore, blest one-in-three
O grant us life that shall not end, in our true native land with Thee.
Amen

Litany of the Holy Angels

Priest: Kyrie Eleison
Congregation: Kyrie Eleison
Priest: Christe Eleison
Congregation: Christe Eleison
Priest: Kyrie Eleison
Congregation: Kyrie Eleison
Priest: Holy Mary, Queen of Heaven
Congregation: Pray for us
Priest: Holy Archangel Metatron
Congregation: Pray for us
Priest: Holy Archangel Raziel
Congregation: Pray for us
Priest: Holy Archangel Tzaphqiel

Congregation: Pray for us
Priest: Holy Archangel Tzadqiel
Congregation: Pray for us
Priest: Holy Archangel Kamael
Congregation: Pray for us
Priest: Holy Archangel Michael
Congregation: Pray for us
Priest: Holy Archangel Haniel
Congregation: Pray for us
Priest: Holy Archangel Raphael
Congregation: Pray for us
Priest: Holy Archangel Gabriel
Congregation: Pray for us
Priest: Holy Archangel Sandalphon
Congregation: Pray for us
Priest: All ye Holy Angels of God
Congregation: Pray for us
Priest: Hosts of the Ashim
Congregation: Pray for us
Priest: Hosts of the Cherubim
Congregation: Pray for us
Priest: Hosts of the Beni-Elohim
Congregation: Pray for us
Priest: Hosts of the Elohim
Congregation: Pray for us
Priest: Hosts of the Melakim
Congregation: Pray for us
Priest: Hosts of the Seraphim
Congregation: Pray for us
Priest: Hosts of the Chasmalim
Congregation: Pray for us
Priest: Hosts of the Aralim
Congregation: Pray for us
Priest: Hosts of the Auphanim
Congregation: Pray for us
Priest: Holy winged Human Angel
Congregation: Pray for us
Priest: Holy winged Lion Angel
Congregation: Pray for us

Priest: Holy Eagle Angel
Congregation: Pray for us
Priest: Holy Bull Angel
Congregation: Pray for us
Priest: Holy Mary, Queen of all Angels
Congregation: Pray for us
Priest: All ye Holy Angels of the God of Hosts
Congregation: Pray for us
Priest: Lamb of God slain from the foundation of the world
Congregation: Help and heal us all
Priest: Lamb of God slain from the foundation of the world
Congregation: Help and heal us all
Priest: Lamb of God slain from the foundation of the world
Congregation: Grant us Peace

Priest: Almighty and Everlasting God, with all our hearts we praise
You for the Celestial Glory of Your ministering Spirits; Archangel
Michael and all Your Holy Angels. We thank You for their wonderful
Wisdom, their Strength, their Radiant Beauty and their irresistible
Power which is utterly used in Your service. Following their example,
we devote our will to do Your Will on earth as it is in Heaven, through
Christ, the King of the Angels

Congregation: Amen

Priest: Eternal God, before Whose Glory the Angels veil their faces.
You have ordained and constituted the services of Angels and
humans in a wonderful order. In Your Love grant that as Your Holy
Angels always serve You in Heaven, so by Your appointment they
may inspire and defend us. We ask this Oh most Holy One,
through Christ, Your Light Within us

Congregation: Amen

(Priest purifies the enthroned Sacrament with incense as the Tantum
Ergo Sacramentum is said or sang)
Priest: "Therefore we before Him Bending, this Great Sacrament
revere, Types and shadows have their ending, for the newer rite is here
Faith our outward sense befriending, makes our inward vision clear,

Glory let us give a Blessing, to the Father and the Son, Honour,
Might and Praise addressing, while eternal ages run, Ever too her
love confessing, who from both with both is one. Amen"

(Priest alone stand and says / sings)

Priest: Thou didst give them bread from Heaven

All: Containing within itself all sweetness

Priest: O Christ, Thou hidden dweller in the human heart

All: Open your eyes in us that we may see!

Priest: O God, Who in this wonderful Sacrament of the altar has
given us a living memorial of your love, help us to venerate the
Sacred Mystery of Your Body and Blood, that we may always see
within us, the Power of Your Indwelling Life. And so by the glad
outpouring of our lives in service, we may know ourselves to be One
with Thee and with all that lives; ever One God throughout the ages
of ages

All: Amen

Priest: To the Mystery of the Holy Trinity - Father, Son and
Holy Spirit + Three in One, to Christ, Son of the Great Light and
the Prince of Peace, and to the Seven Mighty Archangels before
the Throne and to the Holy Assembly of Just Humans-made-perfect,
the Watchers, the Saints, Holy Ones, be praise unceasing from every
living creature, now and evermore

All: Amen

(The Solemn Benediction is now given & after leaving the Temple
in silence)

The Holy Mass of Easter

A.S.A. APOSTOLIC SUCCESSION OF ARIMATHEA

Opening: Priest enters and stands before the altar. A moment of silence.

Invocation

Priest: This is the Day that God has made
Congregation: Let us rejoice and be glad

Priest: I will go up to the Altar of God
Congregation: Even unto the God of my joy and gladness

Priest: Send forth Thy Light and Thy Truth
That they may lead me, and bring me unto Thy Holy Hill,
And to Thy Dwelling Place
Congregation: And I will go up to the Altar of God, even unto
the God of my joy and Gladness

Priest: In the Name of God, the Creator, the + Redeemer and
the Transforming Spirit

All: Amen

(Priest performs Aspergil, three times self, three times the altar and
three times the congregation)

Priest: All Encompassing One, Who ceaselessly creates and sustains,
The fabric of the Universe, send forth Your Holy and beloved Angels,
To guard, encourage, protect and teach all who dwell within this place.
In Your strength Oh God, do we command all adverse powers, to
wither into nothingness; that they shall not abide,
And that our Temples + within, and our Temples + without,
May emerge as strong, pure vessels, to contain the Eternal Mystery,
as it unfolds on earth.

All: Amen

Lighting of the Four candles

Priest: I will kindle my fire this day,
In the Presence of the four Archangels of Heaven;
In the Presence of Raphael, regent of the Air,
In Presence of Michael, regent of the Fire
In Presence of Gabriel, regent of the Waters
In Presence of Uriel, regent of the Earth,

Without malice, without jealousy,
Without envy, without fear,
Without terror of anyone under the sun

All: God, Kindle Thou in my heart within,
A flame of love to my neighbour,
To my foe, to my friend, to my kindred and all,
To the brave, to the knave, to the thrall,
The Blessings of Heaven be upon us,
From the lowliest creature that lives,
To the Name that is Highest of all,
Amen.

Purification

(First censing, invocation of the Angel of Christ)

Priest: Purify this place O God, and make of us One Body,
Growing into the Fullness of Christ,
A Temple of Living Stones, through which Infinite Life may flow,
Let the Angels and Archangels join us in this Work of transforming
the Earth

Addressing penitential rite

Priest: My companions, to prepare ourselves to receive and celebrate
the Sacred Mysteries, let us make our confessions before God

All: Create in me a clean heart, O forgiving Love,
And renew a right Spirit within me

Here is my body, I cast it down before you,
Heal its imperfections with your perfection and make me whole.
Here is my mind, I spread it out before you,
Forgive my foolishness and ignorance with Your bright wisdom.
Here is my heart, it is Yours alone,
Forgive its restless wanderings from You
Here is my life, I offer it unto You,
Do with me as You will, forgive me,
Together with yourself, restore unto me, the joy of Your Salvation,
That I may awake in Your likeness and be satisfied,
Through Christ, the Indwelling Light,
Amen

Absolution

Priest: The Mercy and Grace of God be upon you + will forgive all
our sins and bring us to Eternal Light
All: Amen

KYRIE (spoken by all)
KYRIE ELEISON
KYRIE ELEISON
KYRIE ELEISON
CHRISTE ELEISON
CHRISTE ELEISON
CHRISTE ELEISON
KYRIE ELEISON
KYRIE ELEISON
KYRIE ELEISON

Gloria

Priest: Glory be to God, the Inmost and Most Highest

All: And peace to its people on earth. Almighty God our Father -
Mother,
We worship You, we give You thanks, we praise You for Your Glory,
Christ, all Redeeming One, Son of the Great Light,
Help and heal us all.

You are seated at the Right Hand of the Father, receive our prayer,
For You are the Chief among the Holy Ones, You are the One,
The Beloved Child, who with the Holy Spirit,
Art one in the + Glory of God.
Amen

Collect

Priest: O God of Love, we praise and thank You for this wonderful
feast of Christ's Resurrection. In this Glorious Victory You have
given us a sure and certain witness, that Love and Beauty shall finally
triumph over hate, and that death is but a doorway to the ineffable
Splendor of Eternal Life in You. The never setting Sun of Light;
the Heart of all Brightness

Oh God of Love and Father of Light in Whom there is not darkness at
all; we praise and thank You for this Holiest Mystery of the Resurrection,
for in it is prefigured the time when we too shall be raised in Glory and
serve you, clad in deathless bodies of rainbow light.

And we pray that the Light of the Resurrection may redeem the
nations, dissolve the chains of fear and hatred, and so bring all Your
children into Your Tabernacle. May Your effulgent temple of Peace
shine upon the earth and bless all beings. We ask this through
Christ, the Anointed One, Who is one with You and the Holy Spirit,
the Infinite Breath of Heaven, now and forever.

All: Amen

Liturgy of the word
Readings

Priest: Epistle of Paul to the Corinthians
'Now if Christ be preached that he rose from the dead, how say some
among you that there is no resurrection of the dead? But if there is no
resurrection of the dead, then Christ is not risen and we preach in
vain. So is the resurrection of the dead… it is raised in in-corruption.
It is sown in dishonour, it is raised in glory and sown in weakness.

It is raised in power. It is sown in a natural body and raised in
a spiritual body.... So this corruptible must put on in-corruption
and this mortal must put on immortality. O death where is thy sting?
O grave where is thy victory? Thanks be to God Who giveth us
the Victory through Yahushua - the Christ....'

Priest: This is the Word of God

All: Thanks be to God

Gradual

Priest: Whoever loves Wisdom, loves life; and they that seek her
early, shall be filled with joy. Teach me, O Christ, the Path to Your
Mystery, and I shall keep it unto the end. Give me understanding
and I shall keep Your Law; I shall keep it with all my heart.
For the path of the Just is as the Shining Light, shining more
and more unto that perfect day

Priest: Reading of the Gospel

Invocation: Cleanse my heart and my lips O Most High, Who by
the hand of your Angel-Seraph, did cleanse the lips of your Prophets
with that of a burning coal from Your Altar. And in Your loving -
kindness, purify me, that I may proclaim the Holy Gospel

May the Divine be in my + heart and on my + lips, that through my
heart the Love of God may shine forth and my mouth may manifest
Its Power. Amen

Priest: God be with you

All: And also with you

Priest: This is a reading from the Holy Scriptures

Priest: This is the Gospel according to Mary Magdalena
As it began to dawn towards the first day of the week,
Mary Magdalene and the other Mary came to see the tomb.

And Behold, there was a great earthquake for the Angel of God
descended from Heaven and came and rolled back the stone from
the door of the Tomb and sat upon it. The Angels' countenance was
like lightning and his raiment white as snow and for fear of this
Angel, the keepers did shake and become as dead men. And the
Angel said unto the women: 'fear not, for I know that you seek
Yahushua who was crucified. Why do seek the living among the
dead? He is not here, he has arisen as he said. Come and see the place
where he lay and go quickly and tell his disciples that he is risen
from the dead'. And they departed from the sepulchre with awe
and great joy and did run to bring the disciples word. And as they
went to tell, Yahushua met them on the road, saying: 'All Hail'
and they came and took him by the feet and venerated Him.

Priest: This is the Good News according Mary Magdalena

All: Praise to You O Christ

Sermon (meditation)

As we prepare to meet Christ on the Easter Sunday, I invite you to
lay aside all cares, sink into meditation, and rest in God's Presence,
as we move to the Temple of the Virgin.
Mary guides us to the wall, which leads in from the right side of
the east. The gate in this wall is hung with a curtain of orange,
embroidered with a sword. Mary speaks to us of how a sword pierced
her heart at the crucifixion of Christ, and how love often has to bear
grief, even over losses that are necessary and bring greater Life.

Following Mary through the gate, we are standing at twilight before
an open cave. The other Mary's: Cleopas, Salome, and Magdalene
are here. With great care they anoint our bodies with spikenard.
The pungent smell of the oil is difficult at first, but something shifts,
and we give ourselves over to what is happening. The Mary's sing a
beautiful song of grief as they work. They wrap us in white shrouds
and lay us upon cold stone beds within the cave, before sealing the
entrance. We can still hear the mournful song in the far distance,
as we feel the cold stone and breathe in the thick aroma.

Stillness takes over and we have no idea how long we are in the cave - hours or even days, it could be. Whether conscious or not, we know that, at some deep level, we are journeying through the world of images, with new wisdom finding its way into our souls. The process will continue in the coming days, as our bodies sleep in the outer world.
We blink our eyes as a sharp ray of light intrudes into the dark, silent cave-tomb. A profoundly familiar voice is calling our name. Perhaps it is a name we know, or one that is unknown, and yet even more truly ours. The voice vibrates with a love which envelopes us, and breaks down all illusions, all separations. The light of this word brings life and warmth to the wisdom newly implanted in our souls. We know it is Christ.... And Christ walks into the cave, shining like the noonday sun. Gently giving us its hand and removing our shroud. Christ takes us in a long embrace, and we give ourselves to a love so vast that it shrinks from nothing. As we open our eyes, we are back with Mary, among the roses - where we may remain as long as we wish

Credo

All: (spoken)
I Believe in God the Divine Mystery, beyond all definition and all rational understanding, The Heart of all that has ever existed, that exists now and ever will exist

I Believe in Yahushua, Messenger of God's Word, Bringer of Gods Healing, Heart of Gods Compassion, Bright Star in the Firmament, of Gods Prophets, Mystics and Saints

I Believe in the Holy Spirit, the Life of God that is our innermost Life, the Breath of God moving in our Being, the Depth of God Living in each of us

I Believe that I am called to be Yahushua's Twin, allowing myself to be a vehicle of God's Love, a Source of Gods Wisdom and Truth, and an instrument of Gods Peace in the World

I Believe that Gods Reign is here and now, stretched out all around us for those with eyes to see it, hearts to receive it and hands to make it happen

I Believe in the community of God seekers, in all religions, the prophets, mystics and saints, and those just beginning their Spiritual Journey

I Believe in a future on this earth, when all will be God-centred and God conscious; when we will learn to live in Peace and Love, in the fellowship of brothers and sisters

I Believe that in death life is changed, not taken away and that we will always go, from step to step in Gods Life, Gods Love and Gods Glory for All Eternity. Amen. Amen. Amen

Prayers of the Faithful

Priest: My companions, let us call to mind God's many Blessings and ask to hear the prayers which are inspired to ask

Priest: For all of us gathered in this Holy place, in faith, reverence and love of God That we may offer an acceptable sacrifice
We pray to the Holy One:

Congregation: Most Beloved One, hear our prayer

Priest: For God's Holy Church and every place of worship at this very moment, and all its devotees and those who lead them.
That the Holy One guide and protect them
We pray to the Holy One:

Congregation: Most Beloved One, hear our prayer

Priest: For all our brothers and sisters in need, that Christ assists them
We pray to the Holy One:

Congregation: Most Beloved One, hear our prayer

Priest: For all the peoples of the world, that Christ unites them in peace and harmony
We pray to the Holy One:

Congregation: Most Beloved One, hear our prayer

Priest: For those who serve us in public office and those entrusted
with the common good
We pray to the Holy One:

Congregation: Most Beloved One, hear our prayer

Priest: For those who are in sickness or in suffering, especially
for those who we now name before Thee (read names)
We pray to the Holy One:

Congregation: Most Beloved One, hear our prayer

Priest: For all the departed and those who mourn them.
Especially those whom we now name before Thee (read names)
We pray to the Holy One:

Congregation: Most Beloved One, hear our prayer

Priest: And for any special intention that you may have, said in silent
prayer (pause).... we pray to the Holy One:

Congregation: Most Beloved One, hear our prayer

Priest: Now let us call upon our Heavenly Mother, asking Her to
unite our prayers with Hers, as we say:

All: Hail Mary full of grace, the Beloved and Holy One is with Thee.
Blessed art Thou amongst women, and Blessed is the Fruit of Thy
Womb. Holy Mary, Mother of God, pray for us now, and at the hour
of our victory, over sin, disease and death. Amen

Sign of Peace

Priest: My companions, we have confessed our sins and we have
been forgiven; Christ the Compassionate King, binds us with a bond
of Love that cannot be broken. Therefore in the Name of the Logos
ever present ever saying: "Peace I leave with you, my Peace I give
unto you; not as the world gives do I give it unto you"

The Peace of Christ be always with you
Congregation: And also with you

Presentation of the Gifts

(Priest lifts Shroud from the Grail and Paten)
Priest: Leave the mortal and the temporal to the realm of the world,
for they are as dust and ash, while I am Immortal and Eternal
amongst you. Behold Me as I Am and behold your own face within
Me (presentation Shroud)

(Priest raises Paten)
Priest: Most Holy One, accept that of which by the nature of this
planet we are composed, and in our great gratitude, we offer this
bread unto You, as we likewise offer ourselves

All: On this paten O Christ, with this Bread, we place all the creative
actions of the peoples of the earth, their aspirations, their joy, their
achievements and their work.

Priest: Blessed are You, God of all Creation, through Your Goodness
we have this Bread to offer, which earth has given and human hands
have made
It will become for us, the + Bread of Life.

All: Blessed be God forever

(Priest fills the Cup)
As your Spirit would move the heart of every being,
Now we move water within this wine, and they shall move as one

Priest: We adore you O God, and offer unto You this Water and
Wine, as we offer that which gives us life. From You have we come
and unto You shall we return

All: Into our Chalice with this Wine, we pour the sorrows, the pain
and the suffering of all your creation. Into this offering of the world,
we would gather, those closest to us, those whose lives are bound
up with our own

Priest: Blessed are You God of all Creation, through Your Goodness
we have this Wine to offer, fruit of the vine and work of human hands
It will become for us our + Spiritual Drink

All: Blessed be God forever

Sign of bondage

All: With these we unite those more distant and less familiar to us,
The great multitude of humanity, scattered over every part of the globe,

In deepest sympathy and understanding, we unite ourselves,
With the ceaseless pilgrimage of humanity - past, present and future,
With all its joys and sorrows, its hopes and fears,
That we may be one with it all
We would draw into this offering every form of life; animals, trees,
flowers and fruits, rocks and fire, wind and water, and the very fabric
of the earth itself
We offer ourselves, all that we have and all that we are
Let all Existence be now placed on our altar, that we may raise it up
to Thee

Second censing

(Priest performs the censing of the offerings - Shroud and the
congregation - and lifts Paten and Chalice)
Priest: receive O Source of Life, this Your manifold Creation, in all
its Light and all its Darkness.

All: Amen

Lavabo

Priest: I will wash my hands in innocence O God, and so I will go
to Your Altar

Orate Fratres

Priest: Pray my companions, that our sacrifice may be acceptable to God
Congregation: May the Holy One accept this sacrifice at your hands
and sanctify our lives in Its service

Prayer over the gifts

Priest: Most Holy One, by these Holy Gifts we offer, make + Holy
those who gather in Your Name. May we who share this sacrament,
experience the life and power it promises and enter Your Presence.
All: Amen

Sursum Corda

Priest: Christ, the Anointed be with you
Congregation: And also with you

Priest: Lift up your hearts
Congregation: We lift them up to the Most High

Priest: Let us give thanks to the Holy One
Congregation: It is right to give thanks and praise

Preface

Priest: O Holy One of Blessing, God of all being
We do well always and everywhere to give you thanks
You have no need of our praise, yet our desire to thank You is itself
Your Gift Our prayer of thanksgiving adds nothing to Your Greatness,
but makes us to grow in Your Grace.
You give us Your Holy Spirit, the Comforter, to help us always with
Her Power, so that with loving trust, we may turn to You in all our
troubles and give You thanks in all our joys

Source of life and goodness, You have created all things,
To fill Your creatures with every blessing, and lead all to the joyful
vision of Your Light. Countless hosts of Angels, stand before You, to
do Your Will.
They look upon You, and praise you night and day.
United with them; with Angels and Archangels; with Thrones,
dominations, Princedoms, Virtues and Powers, with Cherubim,
Seraphim and Ashim,
And in the name of every creature under Heaven,
We too praise Your Glory as we say:

Sanctus

All: Holy! Holy! Holy! God of power and might
Heaven and earth are full of Your Glory
Hosanna in the Highest
Blessed are they who come in the Name of the Holy One
Hosanna in the Highest

Canon of the Mass

Priest: Beloved One, You are Holy indeed, the Fountain of all Holiness,
As one family we gather around Your Table,
Here is the Sacrifice of Christ offered in mystery

Here is prepared Christ's table, at which Your children,
Are nourished by the Body of Christ,
Here Your people drink from the Living Spirit,
The stream of living water, that flows from the Stone of Christ
Loving Creator, we bring You all these gifts of Bread + and Wine +

And ourselves as a living sacrifice
Let Your Spirit descend upon these gifts, to make them Holy,
Sanctify them, that they may become,
The Body + and Blood + of Christ,
Who has willed us to make this Eucharist

Consecration

Priest: The day before He suffered He took bread into His sacred hands,
And with His eyes lifted up to Heaven, He gave You thanks and praise.
He broke and + Blessed the bread, giving it unto His disciples, saying:

"Take and eat this all of you, for This is my Body"

When supper was ended, He took this cup into His sacred hands,
Again He gave You thanks and praise. He blessed + the cup,
and gave it Unto His disciples saying:

"Take and drink this all of you, for
This is the Cup of My Blood"

Whenever you do these things I AM is present among you

Affirmation

All: Thee we adore O hidden splendour Thee
Who in Thy sacrament dost deign to be
We worship Thee beneath this earthly veil
And here Thy Presence we devoutly Hail

Priest: Father, we celebrate the Mystery of Christ, we your people and
your ministers, recall His incarnation and Passion, His triumphant
resurrection from the dead and His ascension into Your glory
And from the many gifts You have given us, we offer to You,
God of Glory and Majesty, this Holy and perfect sacrifice-
The Bread + of Life
And the Cup of + Eternal Salvation

Congregation: Look with favour on these offerings and accept them
as once you accepted the gifts of Abraham and Sarah, our parents in
faith, and the wine and bread offered by Your priest - Melchizedek

Priest: Almighty God, we pray that Your Angel may take this
sacrifice to Your altar on High. There to be offered by them, Who as
the eternal High priest, forever offer their lives as the eternal sacrifice

And as He has willed that the heavenly sacrifice shall be mirrored
here on earth, so that Your people may be united more closely to You,
We pray for Your servants, Who minister at this altar,
That by celebrating these mysteries, of the Divine Body + and Blood
+
They may be filled + with Your Mighty Power and Blessing Loving
God, we call You Father, but you are the fountain of Motherhood,
Male and female You created us, in Your own image and likeness.
May all people come to know, that in You, there is no male or female,
No distinction between race, class or colour,
For we are all one within You

All: Through Christ, You give us all these gifts
You fill them with Life and Goodness
You Bless them and make them Holy

Minor Elevation

Priest: By + Him, with + Him, and in + Him,
In the unity of the Holy Spirit,
All Glory and Honour is Yours Almighty God
Forever and ever

All: Amen

Communion rite

All: Our father Who art in Heaven, hallowed be Thy Name,
Thy Kingdom come, Thy will be done, on earth as it is in Heaven,
Give us this day our daily bread and forgive us our trespasses,
As we forgive those who trespass against us, and lead us not into
temptation, but deliver us from evil.
For Thee + is the Kingdom, and the Power and the Glory,
Forever and ever. Amen

Veneration of saints

Priest: Here we give praise to those channels of Your grace;
the Just Ones made perfect: Enoch, Jesus Christ, John the Beloved,
Maria Magdalena, Plato, Plotinus, Clement of Alexandria,
Pythagoras, Jacob Boehme, Meister Eckart.... and any other saints
or teachers that you wish to venerate (Silence)....
And we + join with them before Your Great white Throne. From
which flows infinite Love, Light and Blessing, through all the worlds
that You have made

Fraction

Priest: O Son of God, You show Yourself this day upon countless altars,
Yet, truly remain One and Indivisible,
In token of Your great sacrifice, we break (breaking of the Host) this,
Your Body.
And in token of Your triumph over + death, and the oneness of Your
+ Spirit and Body, and Your Glorious + Resurrection, we unite this
Your Body, with this Your Blood (unite). Praying that by this action,
ordained from old, they may be for us, and for all the world,
a channel of grace and of life Eternal. Amen

Agnus Dei

Priest: Lamb of God, slain from the foundation of the world
Congregation: Help and heal us all

Priest: Lamb of God, slain from the foundation of the world
Congregation: Help and heal us all

Priest: Lamb of God, slain from the foundation of the world
Congregation: Grant us peace

Priest: This is the lamb of God slain from the foundation of
the world, happy are those who take place at His Supper

All: Christ our Passover is sacrificed for us, therefore let us keep
the feast.

As You gave Your Body and Blood, so too I offer myself wholly unto
You. My body and my blood, to transform as You Will, that Your
mystery is completed within me ☥

Communion

(Priest takes communion first then to the congregation)
Priest: Gives out communion saying:
The Body of Christ + and the Bread of Angels,
The Blood of Christ + and the Grail of Eternal Life

Post communion prayer

Priest: I have eaten Your Sacred Body, no darkness will take me,
I have looked upon it, now my eyes see Your wonders,
I have not been a stranger to Your Mysteries,
I am never separated from You ☥

Conclusion

Priest: let us pray
Under the veil of earthly things, now have we communion with
the Beloved Christ. With open face we do see Him, and being made
anew, like unto His own Glorious Body, may we abide in Your
Presence always O God,
And serve You night and day. Amen

Priest: The mystery is complete and the rite is ended and the Blessed
Archangels depart in joy and Peace

All: We give thanks to all the Holy Angels of Heaven and to God
Who send them

Priest: The Blessing of God the Creator, the Redeemer + and
the transforming Spirit. Amen

Priest: Ite Missa est
All: Deo Gratias
☥

Part 4 Clerical Rites and Ceremonies

The Rite of Vesting (vesting prayers)

Washing of hands: Cleanse my hands O God that I may render unto
Thee a pure offering and a perfect work.

Alb: Endue me with the garment of innocence and the vesture of
light that I may receive Thy Gifts and dispense them unto this earth.

Girdle: Bind me to Thee O Christ with the cord of love and the girdle
of purity, that Thy power may dwell in me.
Knot 1: Vilon, knot 2: Rakiyah, knot 3: Shehakim, knot 4: Zebul,
knot 5: Mahon, knot 6: Makom, knot 7: Arabot

Stole: O thou who hast said, "My yoke is easy and my burden light",
grant that I may bear Thy Blessing unto the world.

Chasuble: May the vesture of Grace which I wear and the offering
I am about to make, crown in me a labour of Righteousness and a
Holy Work to the Glory of God and the Angel Hosts. To the joy of
the saints and the salvation of mankind through Christ the Indwelling
Light. Amen.

Cross: O Thou Who of Thy most Holy Will hast hallowed the Sign
of the Cross and made it forever Thine own, let the 7 rays of Thine
Ineffable Glory shine through this sacred symbol, that this Holy
Cross may be a radiant sun unto me and a Fount of Light and benison
to all Thy people. Amen.

Ring (Priest or Bishop): By this token of Eternity and the everlasting
bond of love between God and its creation, I wear this ring as a sign
of that Covenant.

☦

The Blessing of Holy Water

A.S.A. APOSTOLIC SUCCESSION OF ARIMATHEA

Over the Salt
Priest: I exorcise you, creature of salt - by the Living God ✚, by the
Holy God ✚, by the Omnipotent God ✚, that you may be purified by
all evil influences in the Name of the most Holy One, Who is Master
of Angels and Humanity and Who fills all the worlds with Its Glory
and Majesty.
All: Amen

Priest: We pray to you O God, in Your Infinite lovingkindness, to stretch
forth the right hand of Your Power upon this creature of salt, which we
Bless ✚ and Hallow ✚ in your Holy Name. May this salt bring health of
mind and body to all who are touched by it, and wherever it is used, may
every power of adversity and every illusion or working of evil be driven
forth, and abide not, through Christ, the Master of the Elements.
All: Amen

Over the Water
Priest: I exorcise you, creature of water - by the Living God ✚, by
the Holy God ✚, by the Omnipotent God ✚, that you may be purified
by all evil influences in the Name of the most Holy One,
Who is Master of Angels and Humanity and Who fills all the worlds
with Its Glory and Majesty.
All: Amen

Priest: We pray to you O God, for the helping and protection of
humankind and all creation, that You Bless the water set apart for the
Sacred Work to be undertaken. May we come to know Your Infinite
Lovingkindness, and stretch forth the right hand of Your Power upon
this creature of water, which we Bless ✚ and Hallow ✚ in Your Holy
Name. May this water bring health of mind and body to all who are
touched by it, and wherever it is sprinkled make all Holy and Pure.
May every power of adversity and every illusion or working of evil be
driven forth, and abide not, through Christ, the Master of the Elements.
All: Amen

(Priest casts the salt three times in the water in the sign of the Cross
and Circle)

Priest: Let salt and water mingle together in the Name of the Creator
✠ the Redeemer ✠ and the Transforming Spirit ✠ Amen.

Priest: The Peace of Christ be with you
All: And also with you

Priest: Omnipotent Creator, whose Spirit breathed upon the Face
of the Waters and Whose Splendour shines throughout all creation,
have regard for this Your creature of salt and water and pour upon
it the radiance of Your Blessing ✠ and Hallow ✠ it with the Dew
of Heaven, so that wherever it is sprinkled and Your Name invoked,
there may be Your Protection be established and there may your Holy
Spirit abide, You Who Live and Reign with Your Son in the unity
of the Holy Spirit, ever One God throughout the ages of ages.
All: Amen

Baptismal rite

(If this water be used for baptism, the following additional prayer
is also said over the water.)

Priest: O Christ who in the Mystery of Infinite Love took upon
Yourself the limitation of human form; You Who speak the Word that
stills the storm and Who gathers the children into Your arms.
Look upon this sanctified water and fill it with Your Heavenly ✠
Grace and Blessing ✠ so that it may be the shining gate into the new
birth in Your Glorious Body. May all who are baptised with this
water be purified from all influences and seeds of evil and may
Your Holy Angels protect them in all their ways.

Having received the baptism by water, may they come in time to full
spiritual maturity, even unto the baptism by fire and be bathed in Fiery
Light from the Giver of Life, You Who Live and Reign with the Father
in the unity of the Holy Spirit, ever One God throughout the ages of ages.
All: Amen

Solemn Blessing of Oil
of Catechumens by a Priest

A.S.A. APOSTOLIC SUCCESSION OF ARIMATHEA

This solemn benediction must take place during a private votive
Mass, during a public celebration or prior to a Holy Mass, performed
by an Acolyte, Deacon or Priest. Needed is pure olive oil, aloe oil
and Myrrh oil. A suitable storage vessel is set ready. During the Mass
the oil is consecrated after the Presentation of the Shroud and just
before the Presentation of the Gifts.

The Rite

Priest: By virtue of my communion with the Followers of the Way
and the Teachings of Christ and the Apostles known as Joseph
of Arimathea, and the other Grail-Bearers. Together as the servants
of God, I proceed to this Benediction of the Oil of Catechumens.
In the Name of God, I exorcise all influences of evil, and seeds
of chaos, that they may be banished and driven forth from this oil,
which we are about to dedicate to the Divine service.
In the Power of the + Father, the + Son and the Holy + Spirit.

All: Amen

(Taking the consecrated Host between forefinger and thumb, the
priest speaks the words of Blessing, while making the Sign of Power
over the Oil with the Host.)

Priest: In the Power of Christ within all the worlds and invoking the
assistance of the Holy Archangels Michael and Gabriel, I +
consecrate and + Hallow this oil of Blessing, that it may be a spiritual
armour for the safeguarding of the baptized, and that it may be a
vehicle of Heaven's anointing upon the hands of those who are
priests of Christ and the Living Shekinah.

All: Amen

Priest: The Sacred Body of Yahushua was preserved and Blessed through love, dedication and wisdom, and so this Oil was transformed into the Sweat and Tears of Heaven, in which we are nurtured and held for all Eternity.

All: Amen

Priest: Whenever this oil is received by mortal souls, their whole being shall be uplifted and transformed into that of the immortal body of Christ.
Whenever the Holy Fire descends upon them, brought forth by the hand of Christ, the Spirit will accompany the path of this seeker.

All: Now and forever more

(The Host is returned to the Paten, into the Ciborium or Pyx. The vessel of the oil is moved from the altar to a side table or remains there for practical purposes. The Paten and Chalice are then returned to the centre of the altar and Mass is resumed to its conclusion. The oil is preserved in a secure place thereafter)

The Rite of Consecration of the Shroud

This rite must take place during a private and votive mass or during a public celebration only by exception. Needed is the consecrated olive oil with the essential of Myrrh and Aloe. Mass is celebrated as usual until after the Presentation of the Shroud (and possible after making the Holy Oil). After the consecration, the Mass continuous as usual.

The Rite

Priest: As Christ was taken down the cross to be laid down in the Tomb of Arimathea, His Body was prepared with Myrrh and Aloe (takes oil) and His disciples wrapped Him in a linen cloth (takes Shroud in both hands) so they might await the promised Resurrection. And they all bowed down, saying:

All: Amen. Your death is our death and Your resurrection is our resurrection.

Priest: By virtue of communion with the followers of the Way and the Teachings of Christ and the Apostles known as Joseph of Arimathea and the other Grail bearers. Together as the servants of God I purify and consecrate this Holy Relic which Christ gave us - the Sacred Shroud. In the Name of God, I exorcise all evil influences and seeds of chaos, that they may be banished and driven forth from this Shroud, which we dedicate to the Divine service, in the power of the Father ✠ and of the Son ✠ and of the Holy Spirit ✠.

All: Amen

(Priest takes the consecrated Host between fingers and thumb, speaks the Words of Blessing while he makes the sign of the Cross with the Sacred Host)

Priest: In the power of Christ within all the worlds and invoking
the assistance of the Holy Archangels Gabriel and Michael,
I Consecrate ✠ and Hallow ✠ the Shroud made for Christs' Body,
that it may be a spiritual armour for the safeguarding of the disciple.
Let it be the vehicle of Heaven's anointing for those who are priests
of Christ and the Living Shekinah.

All: Amen

(Priest makes four times sign of the cross in all four corners
of the Shroud)

Priest: In the Name of the Holy One + Who is beyond Names and
the Holy Countenance + which is the Face of each expression in
nature. Christ + has given Its countenance to shine through our faces,
now and for all Eternity +

All: Amen

(Priest presents the Shroud to the people and puts the Shroud over its
face in remembrance)

Priest: Emphatah (open yourself)

All: Emphatah. Amen

(Shroud is hung before the Grail and Shield on the altar. Host returns
to Paten / Shield while the oil moves to a side table or altar.
Mass is resumed)

Consecration of the Five Relics

A.S.A. APOSTOLIC SUCCESSION OF ARIMATHEA

The five relics are gathered and brought to the altar. Priest is dressed in white and has Holy Water and Oil prepared. This rite is always done prior to a Holy Mass or separately before any special days. The relics are re-consecrated every month preferably at full moon.

Priest: In the Name of God, the Creator, the ☥ Redeemer and the Transforming Spirit

(Priest puts the Staff horizontally on altar)

Priest: Remember this staff, the implement of the master and the seeker; how Moses directed his authority through the Staff of Miracles, changing it into a mighty snake, resisting the magic of Pharaoh. How he Raised the Divine Power to part the sea for the people to cross, departing for the Land of Milk and Honey. Receive the Holy Water + the Dew of Heaven, and be Empowered and Blessed by the Most Holy One

All: Amen

Priest: Remember the Staff of Yeheshua that was passed on to Joseph of Arimathea and the Followers of the Way. The guiding symbol of the Capax Dei and the token of our devotion to Christ's Teaching. Receive the Oil + that came from the Holy Spirit, and be empowered and blessed by the Most Holy One (Staff is put vertically) proceeding on our way as the Just Ones or the Tzaddekim of our tradition have done; keeping the path straight, maintaining a Greater Order and Peace for all time (Staff is returned)

All: Amen

(Priest takes the Shield and / or Paten)

Priest: Remember this, the Shield of Wisdom and the support and carrier of the Body of Yehoshua. This Shield represents the stone that was rolled before the Tomb of Arimathea; the sepulcher where the body of the Master was resting. Receive the Holy Water + the Dew of Heaven, and be empowered and Blessed by the Most Holy One

All: Amen

Priest: Remember the Shield or Paten during the Sacred Ritual of Christ also called the Eucharist, closing the space where the alchemical transformation will be accomplished and where the resurrection is manifested. This is the Shield that covers the Inner Sanctum of Christ and unveils it when the disciples are open to receive the Eternal Grace. Receive the Holy Spirit through this Holy Oil +

(Shield or Paten is returned)

All: Amen

(Priest takes the Cup)

Priest: Remember this, the Cup of the Last Supper in which the Blood and Water of Yehoshua was poured. This Cup represents the Tomb of Yehoshua, the inner and most Sacred Space for the soul to enter. In here we lay down our lives, to be born again and resurrect together with Christ. Receive the Holy Water + the Dew of Heaven, and be empowered and Blessed by the Most Holy One
All: Amen

Priest: Remember the Cup or the Grail used during the Sacred Ritual of Christ or the Eucharist; the inner temple of final union with God. This is the Grail that all seekers aspire towards and wish to enter, following the example of Christ. The vessel that holds the Body and Blood of the Child of Light. Receive the Holy Spirit through this Holy Oil + (Cup is returned)

All: Amen

(Priest takes the Shroud)

Priest: Remember this, the Shroud of the Dead, in which Yehoshua was wrapped after His crucifixion and suffering. This Shroud preserved the Body of the Master together with the oils of aloe and myrrh. Christ left his face in this cloth for all to see, so that all who follow know that this Face is the countenance of every human soul. Receive the Holy Water + the Dew of Heaven, and be empowered and Blessed by the Most Holy One

All: Amen

Priest: Remember the Shroud, and behold the Face of the Immanent One which is called the Christ, and Who has many names and no name. Look into the countenance of the Father, Who has given us this ancient memory in order that we can see our Creator face-unto-face. The sacred cover over the Vessel that holds the Body and Blood of the Child of Light. Receive the Holy Spirit through this Holy Oil +
(Shroud is returned)

All: Amen

(Priest takes the Cruets)

Priest: Remember this, the Cruets brought by Joseph of Arimathea at the foot of the cross. Herein the Blood and Water from the wound of Yehoshua were caught and preserved. Two streams of Heavenly Dew that became one stream which comes to us as the Mezla or the Grace of God. Receive the Holy Water + the Dew of Heaven, and be empowered and Blessed by the Most Holy One

All: Amen

Priest: Remember the Cruets, and behold the Blood and Water of Christ. Let us take these fluids into our care so we may drink them and become like unto Christ, Who presents the immortality of the Spirit on earth and Who offers us the Essence of Its own Divinity. Receive the Holy Spirit through this Holy Oil +
(Cruets are returned)

All: Amen

Part 5 Ordinations of the Minor & Major Orders of Priest

Ordination of Cleric

Address

Priest: Friends in Christ, the office of Cleric is the first step in
answering Gods call to offered service in the Church and our Temple
on The Way of Christ. This is the beginning of the Alchemy
of Priesthood, the mediation of Gods Glory through all the worlds
and levels of our being.

As physical reality is where much of our conscious experience
begins, so the path of transformation in service begins with the
physical. Those who are called to the order of Cleric offer their
bodies for the manifestation of Christ.
A Work that we call Capax Dei - the readiness to be with God.
Just as Mary offered Her Body for the birth of Yahushua into
this world.

Clerics devote themselves to obedience to God in all aspects of their
everyday lives. Not in any slavish sense, but an inward surrender
which discloses their true nature and vocation. The period of service
as a Cleric is a time of opportunity, a time to step aside from the
plans of the world and turn our attention to the plans of God.
The enfoldment of the Heavens or the Higher Worlds. A time to learn
whether we are ready to leave behind worldly and personal ambition
and offer our time, energy and effort to God on the Way of Christ.
It is a time to remember that our physical body is a temple of the
Holy Spirit, like all other physical forms around us, and that we must
care for these temples wisely so they may be vessels of service
in Purity, Harmony and Beauty.

All: Amen

Priest: let us prepare for meditation

Meditation

As we prepare ourselves to meet the Christ in this blessing today,
I invite you to lay aside all cares and sink deep into meditation
resting in God's nearness. Remember that meditation is God sitting
in Its own Presence.

"We find ourselves in a small room, lit by the soft light of the early
morning. Outside the window, we see the light reflecting off the
white and gold of the nearby temple. A beautiful young woman sits
before us, weaving a cloth of red, purple and blue.

She is concentrated on her work, but looks up as the room fills with
a sense of pressure. Blue and golden light swirl in a column before
the maiden Mary and a voice sounds, as if from the centre of all
things, "Hail Mary…"

The intensity of the Angel's Presence is almost too much for us
and we fail to catch much of Mary's conversation with this Mighty
Messenger. But we see the simple beauty of her wonder at the
Angel's message and catch our breath as the conversation falls into
a moment of waiting silence.

Mary speaks: "Be it done to me according to your word".... and we
hear a deep chord of joy resound through the whole earth.
We feel new life stirring - not only in Mary, but also in our own
bodies. Mary's body begins to radiate with white light, shining like
a Sun, changing the body of Mary in that of an Angel.
Likewise you feel your body transform in that of a Radiant Being - an
Angel. Together with the Virgin we lift our souls in quiet praise...."

Priest: Let those who would offer their bodies and their everyday
lives to God through the office of Cleric, come forward
(candidate comes and sits in a chair before the priest receiving
the Staff of Knowledge in both hands vertically).

Priest: Hold this Staff and hold on tight, for this is the implement
of Knowledge that has been held by many souls of wisdom, like
Abraham and Sarah, Moses, Yeheshua and Joseph of Arimathea,

after which this lineage is named. In the sign and symbol of this Staff,
the Tzaddekim or the Righteous Ones walk the earth in order to keep
all existence and this earth in alignment with the Holy One.

The Vow

Priest: Mary responded to the Angel: "let it be done unto me
according to your word", offering Her body as the vessel of the
incarnation. Jesus prayed in the garden and said: "not my will but
Thy Will be done", offering His Body on the altar of the cross.
Let the same freely offered obedience to God be in you
(a cross is given to the candidate to hold for the duration of
the ordination together with the staff)

All: Amen

Candidate

In the Presence of God and all the Holy Teachers, Saints and Sages,
I vow my obedience to God within and without and in all aspects of
my life. My body shall be a vessel and vehicle for the Transcendent
and Absolute One. May God give me the Grace I need to be faithful.
Amen.

Priest: (points at the cross) So you have chosen to be available to
God in all ways of your life, be reliable unto the Teachings of Christ,
and perform the Work of Capax Dei: to be capable to receive God.
You will be tested on your perseverance, dedication and purity.

Bidding

Let us ask God to bestow upon (name candidate) the Holy Spirit in ever great fullness. May the Spirit keep him / her in constant remembrance of God and give him / her perfect guidance in Holy Service within the world.

Priest:
God the Father-

All: Pour forth Your Love

God the Son-

All: Pour forth Your Love

God the Holy Spirit-

All: Pour forth Your Love

Holy Mary, Mother of Light-

All: Pray with us

All Holy Angels and Archangels-

All: Pray with us

All Holy Orders of Blessed Spirits-

All: Pray with us

All Holy Ancestors and Prophets-

All: Pray with us

All Holy Apostles and Evangelists-

All: Pray with us

All Holy Disciples of Christ-

All: Pray with us

All Priests, Bishops and Confessors-

All: Pray with us

All Holy Teachers-

All: Pray with us

All Holy Saints and the Watchers of God-

All: Pray with us

We pray to you O Christ-

All: Holy One, hear our prayer

Priest: For your church and all who serve within it, that they may be filled with Truth and Love

All: Holy One, hear our prayer

Priest: For this chosen one ✟ that through the Indwelling of Your Holy Spirit, he / she may fulfil his / her ministry

All: Holy One, hear our prayer

Priest: For the Healing of the earth and all Her children

All: Holy One, hear our prayer

Priest: Rejoicing in the fellowship of Holy Mary and all the Saints and Angels, let us dedicate ourselves and our lives unto Christ.

All: To you O God
(Cross and Staff are taken from candidate)

The Ordination

(Priest kneels before the Cleric and anoints his / her feet with Chrism)

Priest: blessed are the feet of those who proclaim the Gospel of Peace. As you begin this path in this lineage that we call The Way, may your feet be blessed, that the walking thereof will bring Grace not only for you, but for the earth and all its creatures.

(Priest / Bishop rises, Cleric kneels)

As a sign of the offering of your physical body unto God and the willingness to leave a former way of life, a tonsure token will now be given (priest / bishop takes a small clip of the candidates hair which is burned immediately. During the candidate recites Psalm 16 or Logion 61 of the Gospel of Thomas)

Priest: Holy One, increase Your virtue in (name candidate), bestowing on him / her the Light of Your Grace ☦
Free him / her from worldly obsessions and remind him / her that we are created in Your Image and Likeness. Help him / her to live joyfully in Your service O great King of Love to Whom be Glory forever and ever.

All: Amen.

(Priest lays hand on Cleric's head)

Priest: Receive the Holy Spirit for the office and work of a Cleric in the Temple of God.

All: May the temple for this Cleric be opened

(Priest clothes candidate in Alb or Surplice)

Priest: (holds the Alb and says) May you be clothed in the habit of Holiness. I admonish you to diligently develop all the powers that are in you, that your service may be of good effect.

This is your new identity and name; dressed in the likeness of an Angel you shall walk the earth, while your soul dwells in Heaven.

Candidate: Endue me with the Garment of Innocence and the Vesture of Light, that I may receive Thy Gifts and dispense them unto this earth.

Priest: (assists in robing the new candidate, saying) You shall be whiter than snow, and thus you're dressed in this Alb, symbol of the Radiant Presence of an Angel.

Priest: (presents girdle or cord, saying) This cord or girdle symbolizes the lineage of this tradition of The Way (around the waste of the candidate)… it signifies the bondage to Christ and the Teachings forthcoming out of this Source (knots are made)… these are the Seven Levels of Spirit, known as the Seven Heavens within Kabbalah (names are told)…. One end of the cord is behind you for those you are going to lead, while the other end is in front of you, held by those teachers and Saints of this tradition who you follow.

Candidate: Bind me to Thee O Christ with the Cords of Love and the Girdle of Purity that Thy Power may dwell within me.

All: Amen

Completion

Priest: (Name) You have received both the opportunities and the responsibilities of the office of Cleric in Gods Holy Temple. You are adopted by the Apostles of The Way who were guided by Joseph of Arimathea in the Name of Christ-Yahushua. In your appearance, your speech and your manner, take care that you always direct the attention of others to God.

May almighty God give you strength, Joy and Endurance for the Work that you have begun.

In the Name of the Father, and of the Son and of the Holy Spirit: Creator, Redeemer and Transforming Spirit ✠ Amen

Ordination of Doorkeeper

Address

Priest: Fellow server in Christ, you have served well in the office
of Cleric and learned to offer your body as God's temple, so that your
outer life can display your inner obedience to God. The Work of
Capax Dei has begun and will continue from this moment on.
You are now called to the order of Doorkeeper who guards the door
for entering and leaving the Sanctuary. Also, the Doorkeeper rings
the Church Bell and holds the Key. Here you will learn that your
emotions are the working power of the Divine Life within you, and
that this power may be raised and consecrated to the service of God.

Such service requires the gift of discernment and the harmonizing
of the warring factions of the soul. As the forces within us come into
balance, we become keepers of the Gate of the Temple of God.
We open the gate to all who seek, letting the Love of Christ flow
through us in selfless service and dedication. For what good is service
when not infused with Love? We also watch carefully, keeping the
gate firmly shut against all hatred, idleness, bitterness and selfishness.

Jesus said that He is the Door, a Passageway, through which we pass as
we journey into God. We become as He is and therefore we will be like a
door for others to pass through, not hindering any soul on its way to God.
Let it be reminded that the sacred hospitality we applied in the Cleric
work, will now be extended upon. Serving faithfully in this order of
Doorkeeper, let us from this day forward open the doors for others and
shut those doors that oppose the Sacred Work that we undertake.

All: Amen

Priest: Let us prepare to go into meditation

Meditation

As we prepare to meet the Christ in this Blessing today, I invite you
to lay aside all cares and sink deep into meditation for a few
moments, resting in God's Presence....

We are walking down a stony street, trying to remember the directions
we have been given, looking for the house where Jesus and his friends
are dining tonight. The evening is drawing on and we start to wonder if
we've taken a wrong turn. But then we notice an unusual collection of
people entering a house just past an upcoming curve in the street...

There is a soldier of the conquering Roman army, a woman with a
particular charisma, an elderly scholar, a slender man carrying some
bags and a few others. We can't see these followers of The Way very
well in this light, but they appear as normal people even somewhat
unclean and shabby. However, we came a long way to be here and
hunger is gnawing at our stomachs and we might as well see who these
people are and if they are followers of the one master we are seeking.

With a bit of nervousness we walk up to the door and knock thrice....
The door opens as we see that it is the master and Teacher - Yahushua,
Who opens the door Himself. He stands before us, flamed in the
flickering light from the candle in the lamp next to the door. He takes
our hands in His, greeting us warmly. Yahushua draws us into the room
where his friends are gathered about a simple table set with bread and
wine. Their gentle eyes meet ours and we know we shall never hunger
or thirst again. As you sit down you are stationed next to the door with
the request to keep an eye on the door and a key is given into your left
hand... than we all hear the Teachings of the Master....

"I am the Way and the Truth and the Life. No one comes to the Father
except through me. We are all passerby. Do not make your home on
the earth, for it is not your place to stay...."
Then, Yahushua holds a disc in front of your face, like looking in
a mirror you catch a glimpse of your higher self... then you hear
knocking on the door of the little house. You open up as the doorkeeper
to receive another soul who wishes to be in the presence of Christ

Priest: Let those who would offer their hearts to God through the office of Doorkeeper come forward.

The Vow

Priest: Yahushua said He came not to be served but to serve, and to give His life as an offering for the many. May this same intention and attitude of service be the central focus of your life, that all power in you may flow out only in Blessing and Love to others. Remember that Christ spoke about God as the Father but also as the One Who is Open. Christ and the Father are as-one and they open the Way for others who follow. Hold on to your Staff and to this Shield or Paten, reminding you of the door that conceals and reveals the Mystery of God (Doorkeeper is given the Staff and Shield or Paten)

Candidate: In the Presence of God; The One-Who-is-Open and all the Holy Ones, I vow that I will serve God and all God's creatures with a heart filled with Joy; loving all creatures as God Loves them. May God give me the Grace I need to be faithful. Amen.

All: Amen

Bidding

Priest: Let us ask God to Bless (name) that she / he may be devoted
night and day to the care of God's inner Temple, frequently
and fervently calling upon the Name of God for assistance.
Let this servant aspire to be in the Presence of the Holy Spirit and
let the Breath of God work through her / him.

God the Father-

All: Pour forth Your Love

God the Son-

All: Pour forth Your Love

God the Holy Spirit-

All: Pour forth Your Love

Holy Mary, Mother of Light-

All: Pray with us

All Holy Angels and Archangels-

All: Pray with us

All Holy Orders of Blessed Spirits-

All: Pray with us

All Holy Ancestors and Prophets-

All: Pray with us

All Holy Apostles and Evangelists-

All: Pray with us

All Holy Disciples of Christ-

All: Pray with us

All Priests, Bishops and Confessors-

All: Pray with us

All Holy Teachers-

All: Pray with us

All Holy Saints and the Watchers of God-

All: Pray with us

We pray to you O Christ-

All: Holy One, hear our prayer

Priest: For your Church and all who serve within it, that they may
be filled with Truth and Love

All: Holy One, hear our prayer

Priest: For this chosen one ✠ that through the Indwelling of Your
Holy Spirit, he / she may fulfil his / her ministry

All: Holy One, hear our prayer

Priest: For the Healing of the earth and all her children

All: Holy One, hear our prayer

Priest: Rejoicing in the fellowship of Holy Mary and all the Saints
and Angels, let us dedicate our life unto Christ and the Father;
the One - Who - is - Openness.

All: To you O God

The Ordination

Priest: Christ, Thou art the Fountain of all Holiness ✠ Sanctify
(Name). Help her / him perform her / his duties with care and thus
receive a share of your treasure. May this candidate be blessed
by Your hand so that she / he may open for others The Way into Thy
Mystery through Christ the master of the Angels, Who reigns with
all of Heaven and is served by all of Hell. Christ, Who is one with
You and the Holy Spirit, now and Eternally.

All: Amen

(Candidate kneels and Priest lays right hand on candidate's head)

Priest: Receive the Holy Spirit for the office and work of
a Doorkeeper in the Church of God and those companions
of the Apostolic succession of Arimathea.

(Candidate returns the Staff and Paten. Priest gives the new
Doorkeeper a Key and a Bell)

Priest: (Name) open your heart for the service of all your
companions, your brothers and sisters, that Christ may Bless them
through you. By the power of Love, ringing through your Life,
summon all people into the service of God. Let the bells ring every
morning to purify the vessels and temples we hold (candidate strikes
bell three times). Open the door with this Key (candidate is given a
key), symbol of Christ for Who no doors are closed, and Who enters
and leaves all places at will.

Be aware Doorkeeper that the Relic of the Paten or Shield that
Arimathea received by Avalake in the desert is a door before the
Shrine or Temple. A door that is placed upon the Holy Cup of Christ.
Know that this shield or door is here to cover or uncover God,
and it is the carrier-plate of Wisdom.

(The new Doorkeeper returns the key and bell and escorts all but the priest out of the chapel. The door is closed and one of the people knocks upon it. The doorkeeper opens the door rings the bell and escorts the people into the chapel. Later: Doorkeeper rings the Bell with the communion that follows in the Eucharist if the ordination is within a Holy Mass.)

(Doorkeeper stands before the people)

Doorkeeper: The Holy One be with you

All: And also with you

Doorkeeper: Enter into the Temple of the Heart

All: We enter therein as you have opened the doorway to it. Amen

(Doorkeeper sits)

Priest: (Name) you have received the office of Doorkeeper in God's Holy Church. May Almighty God give you Strength, Joy and Endurance for the Work you have begun - in the Name of the Father - the Son ✠ and the Holy Spirit.

All: Amen

Ordination of Reader

A.S.A. APOSTOLIC SUCCESSION OF ARIMATHEA

Address: (candidate sits opposite the altar with the Staff)

Priest: Fellow servant in Christ, you have offered your body, your
life and your heart to the Divine for transformation through
the grades of Cleric and Doorkeeper. You are now called to the next
step on this journey, or The Way of Christ's Teachings. The Reader
reads the lessons to the people before the priest expounds on them
and bringing the blessing of the written tradition to the people.
The Reader must also purify the inner worlds so that they may rightly
read the ways of God in the Scriptures, the book of nature and the
book of their own life. Having thus perceived the glory in all things,
they are then charged to proclaim the Spirit of Christ or the Logos to
others. They must be faithful to the Word; that what is read with the
voice is believed in the heart and practiced in deeds, to teach others
by example and make the words come alive.

Priest: Reader, are these things still within the way of your heart?
(answer of the Reader)

Priest: The Reader's mind must be open and pure as a shining Grail,
ready to receive the thoughts of God. In this degree you must put
away unworthy thoughts, remembering that the impure thought arises
with anger, envy, judgement, hate and any other intention that leads
to division and chaos. Do not seek the flaws in the heart of the other
and do not speak about others in their absence. Remain truthful and
honest towards yourself and others, as you have devoted yourself
to this path. Make your thoughts like a clean gem or crystal wherein
is reflected the Beauty and Truth of God. The white Light within
the thoughts of Christ is the inspiration for the Reader. Speak within
the Light of Christ or be silent within that Light.

It is Christ who is our noble example. Let the mind that is in Christ
now be in you ☦ (Staff is returned and a Chalice is given to hold)
Priest: Let us prepare to meditate

Meditation

As we prepare to meet the Christ in this blessing today, I invite you
to lay aside all cares and sink deep into meditation for a few
moments, resting in God's Presence....

We are in a room deep within a temple complex. The walls stretch
high above us and we feel the cool stones beneath us. It is day but
the windows are too small to give us a clear view, while smoky lamps
give additional light.

We are sitting in a gathering of religious scholars, elderly men who
devoted their lives to plumbing the depths of Gods revelation, and
search into the inner temple of the heart. You see their fingers search
their way across the crumbling scrolls. At the door of this scenery
you see a young boy standing in the room. His eyes are sparkling
with light from the high windows. One of the old men asks:
"Son are you lost"? The boy answers in calm assurance:
"I am in my Father's House. The young Yahushua walks into
the centre of our gathering. Isaiah's words flash across our minds....
"And a little child shall lead you all...."

The boy begins to speak, drawing aside the veil of our minds and
revealing the mysteries of the living Word. He says when looking at
the ceiling: "When you know Me you will know the Father and when
you know the Father through Me, you shall be Me as you are the
Father" .... Tears of awe and joy shine in the eyes of the scholars.

We listen with all our being for what the child has to say to us.
We let his words reach deep within our minds and hearts and we rest
in that depth for a few moments...... then we have a vision of a
Golden Chalice that radiates in all directions, the essence within
it overflowing and giving a Blessing to all who are touched by it.

Priest: Let those who would offer their minds and hearts to God
through the office of reader come forward (Reader returns the
Chalice and is placed before the altar with hands on the surface)

The Vow

Priest: Yahushua said: "Blessed are the pure of heart, for they shall see God". If your heart and mind are truly pure, singular in dedication, you shall see God and know the Way. Let your thoughts become vehicles of Divine consciousness; subtly carrying messages from Heaven unto the earth.

Candidate: In the Presence of God and all the Holy Ones, I vow purity in heart and mind, that I may see with the single eye of Spirit, and thus be a trustworthy guide to all who seek the Way. May God give me the Grace I need to be faithful. Amen.

The Bidding

Priest: (Name), you have been chosen to serve as a reader in God's Sanctum and in the companionship of Arimathea or the followers of the Way. We now pray that the Almighty Living One may increase the Grace within you, give you awe and courage and achieve in you all that is needed to fulfil your office as a reader.

All: Amen

Priest: God the Father

All: Pour forth Your Love

God the Son

All: Pour forth Your Love

God the Holy Spirit

All: Pour forth Your Love

Holy Mary, Mother of Light

All: Pray with us

All Holy Angels and Archangels

All: Pray with us

All Holy Orders of Blessed Spirits

All: Pray with us

All Holy Ancestors and Prophets

All: Pray with us

All Holy Apostles and Evangelists

All: Pray with us

All Holy Disciples of Christ

All: Pray with us

All Priests, Bishops and Confessors

All: Pray with us

All Holy Teachers

All: Pray with us

All Holy Saints and the Watchers of God

All: Pray with us

We pray to you O Christ

All: Holy One, hear our prayer

Priest: For your church and all who serve within it, that they may be filled with Truth and Love
All: Holy One, hear our prayer

Priest: For this chosen one ✠ that through the Indwelling of Your Holy Spirit, he / she may fulfil his / her ministry
All: Holy One, hear our prayer

Priest: For the Healing of the earth and all Her children
All: Holy One, hear our prayer

Priest: Rejoicing in the fellowship of Holy Mary and all the Saints and Angels, let us command ourselves and all our life unto Christ, the Indwelling Light.

All: To you O God

The Ordination

(Priest: Anoints the temples of the candidate with Chrism)
Priest: Most Holy One, you are Eternal Wisdom and You hold us safely in Your Embrace. Instruct and improve Your servant (name). Illumine his / her mind with Your Light and give him / her courage and discernment to read and meditate upon Your Word, to the Praise and Glory of Your Name, now and eternally.

All: Amen.

Priest (prayer): Most Holy One, You are the Fountain of all Holiness ✠ (with oil) sanctify (name) that (s)he may become a reader in Your Holy service. May you (name) remind others that Gods reverberation is within all forms of life. That all words are Holy when pronounced with the highest intention.
Help this soul to read what You would have him / her to do, and to do what is being read from the Scriptures, so that (s)he becomes an example of Holiness, through Christ, the indwelling Light who is one with You and the Holy Spirit, one life forever and ever.

All: Amen.

(Candidate kneels and priest lays right hand on candidate's head)

Priest: receive the Holy Spirit for the office and work of a reader in the Sanctum of God and within the Apostolic Succession of Arimathea.

New reader reads from the Wisdom of Solomon (7:22 - 8:1)

The Nature of Wisdom

"There is in Her a spirit that is intelligent, holy, unique, manifold,
subtle, mobile, clear, unpolluted, distinct, invulnerable,
loving the good, keen, irresistible, beneficent, humane, steadfast,
sure, free from anxiety, all-powerful, overseeing all, and penetrating
through all spirits that are intelligent, pure, and altogether subtle.

For wisdom is more mobile than any motion;
because of Her pureness She pervades and penetrates all things.
For She is a breath of the power of God,
and a pure emanation of the glory of the Almighty;
therefore nothing defiled gains entrance into Her.
For She is a reflection of eternal light,
a spotless mirror of the working of God,
and an image of his goodness.

Although She is but one, She can do all things,
and while remaining in Herself, she renews all things;
in every generation She passes into holy souls
and makes them friends of God, and prophets;
for God loves nothing so much as the person who lives with wisdom.
She is more beautiful than the sun,
and excels every constellation of the stars.
Compared with the light She is found to be superior,
for it is succeeded by the night,
but against wisdom evil does not prevail.
She reaches mightily from one end of the earth to the other,
and She orders all things well"-

Priest: So shall it be
All: In our days to come. Amen

Completion

Priest: (Name) you have received the office of reader in Gods Holy
Service. May Almighty God give you strength, joy and endurance for
the work you have begun, in the Name of Father, the Son ✠ and the
Holy Spirit. Creator, Redeemer ✠ and Transforming Spirit. Amen.
Reader is given a Bible or other sacred book as a token of his / her office.
(If received during Holy Mass, the reader will read the Gospels)

Ordination of Healer & Exorcist

Address: (candidate sits opposite the altar with the staff and offers
the written credo to the priest in silence)

Priest: Fellow servant in Christ, you have placed your body, your life
and your heart into the Divine Crucible of transmutation in
the preceding degrees. You are now called to an order known both as
Healer and Exorcist, for those who serve us in this stage of the inner
work and call upon the Grace of the Holy Spirit and thereby
replacing darkness and fear with hope and peace.

The Healer holds God's children in the Light: in that wholeness
which is desired by the Heavenly worlds for each one of us.
The healer lays on hands with prayer, anoints with blessed oil and
pours out the water needed for the Divine service. The act of
devotion is appropriate for this grade and order, leading the candidate
to the uncovering of his own needs and desires, and wilfully directs
oneself to the Higher worlds and God. This needs to be done through
the free will of the newly initiated in this degree. Placing yourself in
the middle pillar, between the mighty columns of dual manifestation,
the healer-exorcist arrives at the narrow and straight path in-between.
This is a practice rather than an achievement. Remember who is
walking in front of you on this middle path. The Christ is your
doorway and the Shroud is the reflection of your face in the Eternal
Image of the Redeemer.

(Priest presents the Shroud to the candidate)

Priest: It is the will which must be strengthened and aligned with the truth
upon this middle road, which leads straight to the Good, the Beautiful and
the True. The staff you are holding is a reminder of this middle path.

We cast out from ourselves the evil inclinations that make us to work
against the all-nurturing and sustaining unity and love in existence.
All that makes us to separate the worlds within: our selfishness is

turned into dedication and devotion to God and the unity within the graceful embrace of the Divine. Open yourself to Healing and Peace, now that you are starting to lift the suffering of the world.
Are you ready to be tested on this middle path, where you may find the greatest Light and find the greatest shadow, in order that your honesty and integrity may come out as pure shining crystals?

Candidate: answer candidate....

Meditation

As we prepare to meet the Christ in this blessing today, I invite you to lay aside all cares and sink deep into meditation for a moment, resting in God's Presence…

We are standing by a dusty road with many others, waiting for Yahushua who is said to arrive here soon. Each of us feels our infirmity in some way, the suffering that seems inherent in living, an inner discomfort we can never seem to completely unknot. We don't know why we believe this teacher can help us, but nonetheless we are here, waiting....

The noise and movement of the crowd signal Yahushua's approach.... There are so many people; how will Yahushua even know we are here? We are almost swept away by the mob, all trying to get a glimpse or even touch the great teacher and healer. Suddenly the crowd opens and without even thinking we reach through, touching the Garment of the Master.

At the moment we touch Him, a tremendous power flows through us and we feel suffused with peace, forgiveness and healing on different levels. We know the truth of who we are as beloved children and the truth of who we may become. Yahushua turns, looks you straight in the eye with deep compassion and smiles at you. It is as if the crowd has melted away and the only thing you see is Him.

He says: "Your faith has healed you.... now go in Peace...."

For a few moments, we let that deep Peace overflow us, pouring out
unconditionally into our bodies and into the world (bell sounds)....

Priest: Let those who would offer up themselves, in order to become
expressions of the Will of God, through the office of Healer,
now come forward

(Candidate comes forward, standing before the altar, touching and
holding the corners of the Shroud of Christ)

The Vow

Priest: Yahushua would not quench burning flax, or bend a bruised
reed. He counselled us to let the wheat and tares grow together.
He told Peter to put away his sword as he healed the wound which
Peter had inflicted. Let the Kingdom of Peace be displayed in your
life. May your life from this day forward bring forth the fruits from
the Garden of Eden. Should this place be the centre of your life,
let all who are with you, be healed and comforted.

Candidate: In the Presence of God and all the Holy Ones, past,
present and future, I vow that I will be a channel of Peace and will
renounce all violence and hatred in thought, word and deed.
All that defiles my heart shall be transformed into spiritual actions
and brought into the world. I will seek Peace and follow after it,
becoming a steward of the Kingdom of Heaven. May God's Spirit
renew the earth and may God give me the Grace I need to be faithful.
Amen

(Candidate let's go of the Shroud and takes his / her seat again)

The Bidding

Priest: Let us ask God to bless (name) that (s)he may be a spiritual vessel and a healer unto the Sacred Kingdom. Let us also pray that this soul will transform into a defender of the Holy and True, so that the duty of exorcism will cast out the pure darkness of this world and restore hope and peace. Pray with me, all here present that (name) shall be guided and assisted by the Choirs of Angels and Archangels of Heaven who are occupied with healing and exorcising evil.

Priest: God the Father-

All: Pour forth Your Love

God the Son-

All: Pour forth Your Love

God the Holy Spirit-

All: Pour forth Your Love

Holy Mary, Mother of Light-

All: Pray with us

All Holy Angels and Archangels-

All: Pray with us

All Holy Orders of Blessed Spirits-

All: Pray with us

All Holy Ancestors and Prophets-

All: Pray with us

All Holy Apostles and Evangelists-

All: Pray with us

All Holy Disciples of Christ-

All: Pray with us

All Priests, Bishops and Confessors-

All: Pray with us

All Holy Teachers-

All: Pray with us

All Holy Saints and the Watchers of God-

All: Pray with us

We pray to you O Christ-

All: Holy One, hear our prayer

Priest: For your church and all who serve within it, that they may be
filled with Truth and Love
All: Holy One, hear our prayer

Priest: For this chosen one ✠ that through the Indwelling of Your
Holy Spirit, he / she may fulfil his / her ministry
All: Holy One, hear our prayer

Priest: For the Healing of the earth and all Her children
All: Holy One, hear our prayer

Priest: Rejoicing in the fellowship of Holy Mary and all the Saints
and Angels, let us command ourselves and all our life unto Christ,
the Indwelling Light.

All: To you O God

The Ordination

(Priest anoints the temples of the candidate with Chrism)

Priest: Holy One, You are Eternal Wisdom and You hold us safely
in Your Embrace. Instruct and improve Your servant (name).
Illumine this soul's heart with Your Light and give him / her courage
and discernment to heal and pray in order to know Your Heart.
To the praise and Glory of Your Name, now and eternally.

All: Amen

Priest: God of Hosts ✢ sanctify (name). Help this soul so that by
anointing and laying on of hands, together with words of inspiration
and faith, (s)he may invoke Your power over all darkness and fear.
May (s)he be a worthy physician of souls in Your Holy Community,
confirmed by Your Gift of healing and a Heavenly Life, through
Christ Who is One with You, One God throughout the ages of ages.

All: Amen.

Priest (prayer): Christ, the fountain of all Holiness ✢ (with oil)
sanctify (name) that (s)he may become a Healer-Exorcist in Your
Holy service. May you remind others that God's Heart is within all
forms of life. That all is love, light and compassion, and is Holy
when seen with the highest intention. Help and aid this soul to make
of life one extended prayer, so that (s)he becomes an example
of Holiness, through Christ, the Indwelling Light who is one with
You and the Holy Spirit, one life forever and ever.

All: Amen

(Candidate kneels and priest lays right hand on candidate's head)
Priest: receive the Holy Spirit for the office and work of a Healer
- Exorcist in the Sanctum of God and within the Apostolic
Succession of Arimathea.

(Candidate rises and receives a dagger or sword)

Priest: Receive this blade, a sign of the power of the will. Do not turn it outwards, in the direction of others in violence or threat. Rather turn it downwards, transfixing the chaos within and directing the evil inclinations of yourself towards unity and harmony. Give all its proper place in the Holy Order of existence (sword or dagger is returned)

Healer-Exorcist reads from Symeon 'the new theologian'

(candidate stands at the altar facing the people)
This text is called: 'We awaken in Christ's body'

We awaken in Christ's body,
as Christ awakens our bodies,
and my poor hand is Christ, He enters
my foot, and is infinitely me.

I move my hand, and wonderfully,
my hand becomes Christ, becomes all of Him,
for God is indivisibly whole, seamless in His Godhood.

I move my foot, and at once,
He appears like a flash of lightning,
Do my words seem blasphemous?
Then open your heart to Him.

and let yourself receive the one,
who is opening to you so deeply,
For if we genuinely love Him,
we wake up inside Christ's body.

where all our body, all over,
every most hidden part of it,
is realized in joy as Him,
and He makes us, utterly, real.

and everything that is hurt, everything,
that seemed to us dark, harsh, shameful,
maimed, ugly, irreparably damaged,
is in Him transformed.

and recognized as whole, as lovely,
and radiant in His light,
he awakens as the Beloved,
in every last part of our body.

(candidate returns to the chair)

Priest: You will receive your new curriculum which includes many
prayers and blessings for the sick and suffering. You will now receive
the oil of blessing that you may use for yourself and others. Use it
wisely, for blessings are not only for those who suffer, but also for
those who are silent and invisible.

This is the oil (gives sacred oil) that we use in the Apostolic
Succession of Arimathea, to ordain the disciple and to hallow and
bless the Shroud of Christ. The Shroud is the new relic for the priest
in this stage of Healer-Exorcist. Remember that the Shroud is shown
in memory that we are all a reflection of God the Transcendent, made
and formed in the Divine image and likeness. The Shroud is also
the cloth that heals and regenerates. It refers to the Robe of Christ
and the physical body that we wear, which is a blessing since the day
of birth, for it contains the capacity to heal. Remember Healer;
this body that was given to you, which was not born to die,
but born to become a vessel for God and all the Higher worlds and
Angels therein.

(Shroud is shown right in front of the face of the candidate. Bell sounds)

Priest: Receive the authority to anoint with oil which has been
blessed for the relief and refreshment of body and soul, and to lay on
hands for inward anointing by God's Holy Spirit. From this day
forward you shall take on the work of preparing the Oil for the Holy
Mass and consecrate the Shroud. The Capax Dei continues in this
dedicated work of the heart.

Besides the gift of the Dagger, Shroud and the Oil, you shall receive
a third and last gift in this ordination. Hold out your right hand,
which is the hand of giving out blessing, and receive this Rosary
which is the tool for praying the worlds into existence.

(Name) you have received the office of Healer-Exorcist in God's
Holy Community and the Apostolic Succession of Arimathea.
May the Divine give you strength, joy and endurance for the work
you have begun. In the Name of Creator, the Redeemer ✚ and
the Transforming Spirit. Go forth in Purity and Devotion.

All: Amen

Ordination of Acolyte

A.S.A. APOSTOLIC SUCCESSION OF ARIMATHEA

(preparation: candidate has confessed in the presence of a priest or bishop)

Address: (candidate sits opposite the altar with the Staff and Shroud covering face until the priest instructs otherwise)

Priest: Fellow servant in Christ, as you have grown and served through the preceding orders, you have aligned body, heart, mind and will to the Divine.

As God's Grace suffuses all levels of our being, the worlds within you are touched by the Glory or Kavod of the Holy One.
The darkness of the self-centered obsessions is lightened with a growing transparency. You will only find the Light of Christ within your own being first. The mystery of the order of Acolyte is the conscious bearing of this Light, being a vessel and a lamp of God's Presence within the world.

To the living of this Mystery you are now called. The duties of the Acolyte are to tend and carry the fires and to present the pure and living waters and wine for the Eucharistic Sacrifice.
The Cruets are the relics of the Acolyte, concluding to the last of the relics in this lineage of Arimathea. From this moment on, you will built up the temple and the altar. Remove the veil of the world and begin to see the Spirit within creation.

Priest: Candidate, remove the Shroud from your face

(Candidate removes Shroud and gives it to the Priest)

Priest: Bear within you the Light of Christ and strife to kindle a sense of that Holy Presence and fire within others (central candle of the altar is given to the candidate)

Priest: It is your duty to see from this day on, the Light within all other creatures, whether they are mineral, vegetable, animal, human or angel. However dark the world may appear to you, or how it presents itself to your ordinary perception.

Having learned to recognize the Light both within ourselves and in others, we are gifted to help them to allow the radiance of the indwelling Spirit to shine forth in pristine Glory and Splendour, until the Light within you becomes one with the Light of the Transcendent God.

All: Amen

Priest: Acolyte! You cannot be a child of Light and serve the darkness. The fruits of Light are Goodness, Justice and Truth. When we live Holy lives, we do good works and offer ourself to God, in order to let our Light shine. You were once darkness, but now you are Light. Walk as a Child of Light!

(Candidate walks towards the altar and returns flame)

Candidate: I and the Father are One

Priest: Acolyte, take your rosary and pray for the darkness to teach you, and become a beacon for the world, revealing the Shekinah, so you may walk in the footsteps of Christ.

(Acolyte kneels at the altar with rosary and prays in silence to the Shekinah)

Priest: Rise Acolyte and be seated and listen to the meditation describing the journey of this order (acolyte sits on the appointed chair)

Meditation

As we prepare ourselves to meet the Christ in this blessing today,
I invite you to lay aside all cares, and sink deep into meditation,
resting in God's presence....

It is early morning and we are walking up a stony hill called Tabor
with Yahushua and some of the other disciples. In this moment with
the soft beginning of dawn on the eastern horizon, we are walking in
quiet companionship. At the top of the hill, Yahushua robed in a
seamless white garment, turns to face us. The sun has just risen above
the horizon behind him and at first we think we are only seeing
the morning light of the sun. Something seems to be wrong with our
vision and our ability to focus becomes difficult and a rainbow
spectrum of light plays before our eyes. We look up and our vision
clears as our eyes adjust to the otherworldly radiance that appears
from all sides.

Yahushua stands before us with arms outstretched, shining with a
brilliant white Light in such brightness that the sunlight behind him
fades away. Our legs give out beneath us, and we fall to the ground.
We look up and can't see Yahushua, but only this beautiful source
of Light.... then Moses and Elijah the prophet stand on either side of
Christ, speaking with him. We utter words of praise in this moment
and our impulse is to build three shrines or altars on the spot. As we
are praying, a shining cloud descends upon us all, and a voice comes
over us, who says: "This is my Son, my Child, the Beloved One.
Hear Him".

Fear overtakes us and we shut our eyes and tremble in God's
Presence. Then we feel a touch on our shoulder and notice that
Yahushua is giving us his hand to lift us. He says: "Arise and have
no fear… you are the Light of the world… let your light shine"…
Finding the Light of Christ within ourselves, we let it radiate
brilliantly through us for a few moments, shining like a sun over
our companions and down the hill of Tabor over the world below.
We hear the final words: "As I was in the beginning, I am now
and will ever be".

Priest: let those who would purify themselves, and offer their lives to God through the office of Acolyte come forward (Acolyte rises and stands before priest)

The Vow

Priest: In the Holy Scripture we are told…"you are no longer foreigners and aliens, but all citizens of God's people and members of God's household, built upon the foundation of the Apostles and Prophets, with Christ himself as the cornerstone."

Like Joseph of Arimathea and the disciples of Christ; they walked away from the darkness and brought the sublime Teachings into the world. Now see and behold your Light and let the Teaching of Christ enter you. Dedicate yourself to this sacred Quest, and let not the darkness ever separate you from God and its creation.

Candidate: In the Presence of God and all the Holy Angels, I vow that I will always regard all people and creatures as my brothers and sisters in the one Light of Christ. May God give me the Grace I need to be faithful.

All: Amen

The Bidding

Priest: Let us ask God to Bless (name) in order that this soul carries
before him / her a visible light, that may shine forth a Spiritual Light.
And as this Acolyte presents pure wine and water at the altar,
so does this soul presents her / himself as a pure and Holy offering
to God. Every step that you take, every inner and outer action, will
be performed in the Light of the Holy One.

Know that you are filled and truly moved by the Holy Spirit. Pray
with me, all here present that (s)he shall be guided and assisted by
the Choirs of Angels and Archangels of Heaven who are occupied
with bringing the Teaching upon the earth and to all its creatures....

Priest: God the Father-
All: Pour forth Your Love

God the Son-
All: Pour forth Your Love

God the Holy Spirit-
All: Pour forth Your Love

Holy Mary, Mother of Light-
All: Pray with us

All Holy Angels and Archangels-
All: Pray with us

All Holy Orders of Blessed Spirits-
All: Pray with us

All Holy Ancestors and Prophets-
All: Pray with us

All Holy Apostles and Evangelists-
All: Pray with us

All Holy Disciples of Christ-
All: Pray with us

All Priests, Bishops and Confessors-
All: Pray with us

All Holy Teachers-
All: Pray with us

All Holy Saints and the Watchers of God-
All: Pray with us

We pray to you O Christ-
All: Holy One, hear our prayer

Priest: For your church and all who serve within it, that they may
be filled with Truth and Love
All: Holy One, hear our prayer

Priest: For this chosen one ✠ that through the Indwelling of Your
Holy Spirit, he / she may fulfil his / her ministry
All: Holy One, hear our prayer

Priest: For the Healing of the earth and all Her children
All: Holy One, hear our prayer

Priest: Rejoicing in the fellowship of Holy Mary and all the Saints
and Angels, let us command ourselves and all our life unto Christ,
the Indwelling Light.
All: To you O God

The Ordination

Priest: Most Holy One, through Christ-Yahushua, you send your
Light into the world, to shine upon and nurture us. Sanctify ✚(name),
help and aid her / him to light the lights in the temples and shrines,
and within the hearts of the congregation.
Let her / him carry the vessels of wine and water, like Joseph of
Arimathea did after the sacrifice of Yahushua on the cross.
Guard an protect her / him, through Christ, who is one with you
and the Holy Spirit, now and eternally.

All: Amen

(Candidate kneels. Priest lays right hand on candidate's head)

Priest: Receive the Holy Spirit, that you may be filled with Light and
serve as an Acolyte in the meeting-place of God.

(Priest gives candle to Candidate)

(Candidate passes it to every person present)

Candidate: "Have no fear, you are the Light of the world.
Let your Light shine"

(Priest takes the candle and gives the cruets from the altar)

Priest: Pour out your life in union with the Great Sacrifice by which
the world is maintained.

Candidate: "This is the Spiritual evidence that the Living Spirit is
amongst us and lives through us. God pours its Grace and Blessing
upon the world and the whole universe. All is bathed in the Glory
of the Holy One from birth to death and the time in-between".

(Cruets are returned to the altar)

Duties

Acolyte: In the Order or Acolyte the act of Confession is introduced
in an inward - and outward way. Truth and honesty in our current
actions are central, but also all the actions that we have performed in
our past that have caused a trail of 'unholy' consequences. This path
of confession is to close the 'streams through which old energies are
wasted'. We lose energy through channels that are unhealthy or even
abusive to our own (Holy) nature. Therefore we need to close those
open channels and streams, before they cause greater damage to
ourselves and others. The streams of the Higher worlds however,
are opened and cultivated through the work of Capax Dei.

Priest: The work for the Acolyte is to confess our ways that have led
to opening and sustaining the wrong channels, and re-opening
the streams of Spirit.
We open the Cup or Chalice of our hearts and clean the inside for
the Higher waters to flow through. Confession is the way of self-
knowledge, where we offers ourselves through honesty and integrity.

Priest: Are you willing and ready to hear the confessions of other
souls in order that they may be healed?

Acolyte: I am open to the world of other seekers, and will care for
them like Yahushua opened himself for the hearts of others. I will
listen and counsel them so they can move on their way towards God.

Priest: Furthermore, blessed companion, you will from this day take
care of the incense and thurible during the sacramental rites.
The fires of the temple are now your responsibility and we will rest
assured that they will be lit and burning for the Holy Mass during
the time of your duties.

Acolyte: So I will. Amen

All: Amen

Completion

Priest: (name) You have received the office of Acolyte in the lineage
of the A.S.A. and the authentic Teachings of Christ.
May the Almighty Living One give you strength, joy and endurance
for the work you have begun, in the Name of the Father, the Son ✝
and the Holy Spirit, Creator, Redeemer and Transforming Spirit.

All: Amen

Ordination of Deacon

Address: (candidate sits opposite the altar with the Staff and Shroud covering face until the priest instructs otherwise)

Priest: Fellow servant in Christ, you have gathered the relics on the Way of Christ and brought them to the Sanctuary where the Ritual of Yahushua is celebrated. What shall you offer to this altar, disciple of Christ?

(Shroud is removed by the priest)

Acolyte: I have received the Staff when ordained as a Cleric, my robes and cord were my only cover during the night;

Next I found a Key and a Paten or Shield on which to carry the Teachings and close the Tomb of Yahushua while being the Doorkeeper of the temple;

When ordained as a Reader, the Grail or Chalice was offered, in which to receive the body and blood of Yahushua;

The Healer-Exorcist ordination provided me with the Knowledge of the Heart, presenting to me the Shroud of our Teacher and the Rosary of prayer:

The Cruets with Blood and Water came from the hands of Joseph of Arimathea, offering me the final relic to transmit the Ritual of the Last Supper.

Priest: You have walked in the Way of Joseph of Arimathea and the other disciples. What is your personal sacrifice on this path?

Deacon: (answers)

Priest: Let it be so. Now let us pray:

O Gracious God, the Seraphim stand before Your Heavenly Sanctuary, veiling their faces and crying out: "Holy, Holy, Holy! Who stands in Your midst is a disciple between Heaven and earth and we now bring You this brother / sister, who stands at the portal of Your earthly Sanctuary, offering him / herself to serve as a Deacon in Your Holy Service and its Universal Church.

May this soul faithfully guard the Gate of Your Mysteries and proclaim Your Holiness in their life.

Through Christ, Your Son, our Teacher and liberator, Who is one with You and Your Holy Spirit, now and eternally.

All: Amen

Address

(candidate is given the Divine Flame of the altar to hold)

Priest: Fellow-server in Christ, the order of Deacon is a grade of probation for the major orders of Priest and Bishop. It gives to us who receive it greater strength and steadfastness of purpose to the end that, with singleness of heart we may dedicate our lives to Christ in His Holy Sanctuary. If before this step we have been remiss in our spiritual practice, we must now be diligent. If we have been drowsy, we must now be alert. If we have been prone to excess, we must now be temperate. If we have behaved dishonourably, we must now be pure and work towards the deepest integrity and truthfulness ☦

So great is the responsibility of the Major Orders and the office of priest, that this grade is given so we may test our dedication. No one gains by entering lightly or unadvisedly upon so solemn an undertaking.

The duties of the Deacon are to guard the gates of the Sanctuary, read the appointed Epistles and Gospels, to present the Chalice or Grail and lay the Paten with bread at the appointed place, prepared for the sacrifice on the altar. You shall wash the altar linen as you wash your soul clean before every Sacrament. Strive always to minister at the Divine Sacrifice in the invisible Sanctuary of our hearts and gather with the Company of the Light and all the faithful ones here assembled. So you will prepare to lead the Mass in your private temple.

We will invoke God's Blessing upon you as you lay yourself as
a Holy oblation in the Presence of Christ ✠

(Divine flame is returned to the altar and the platter with the relics is placed on the side altar)

Meditation

As we prepare ourselves to meet Christ in this blessing today, I invite you to lay aside all cares and sink deep into meditation, resting in God's Presence....
We are gathered with Yahushua and some of His disciples, sitting outdoors in the warm sun.... people have come, talking to the Master, challenging Him, requesting His blessing. We listen carefully to His voice, as all His words seem as much for us as for the inquirers.

A young man in fine clothes approaches Yahushua and we see a true reverence in his bearing. He asks with earnestness: "good teacher, what must we do to be saved"? Yahushua answers, recounting the Commandments and keeping the Covenant given to the people. The man replies: "but I have kept all these precepts from my youth, and still...."
We feel the frustration of the young man. How could all this goodness, all this religious observance still leave a shadow upon the heart?

Yahushua looks at the young man with such deep compassion and love that all around can feel it. We are all one within our vulnerability before such love. Extending his hands to the man, Yahushua speaks....
"you lack only one thing…sell all that you have and give it to the poor and let your treasure be in Heaven. Come and follow me"!

The young man's face falls and walks away. Yahushua turns to us and says: "How hard it is for those with riches to enter the Kingdom of Heaven or for those with power to give it away to the One Who is Openness… it is easier for a camel to pass through the eye of a needle".

Knowing our own clinging to possessions both inner and outer, we ask...."who then can be saved"? and Yahushua replies, "with God all things are possible". Then the Master gives a blessing to all present in this moment, feeling the Presence of Christ with us, giving hope in the possibilities the Spirit provides for us, we ponder all those things that prevent us from passing through the eye of the needle....☧

Priest: Let all those who offer their lives to the service of God's Holy Presence and the Sanctuary of the Holy Spirit, through the office of Deacon, come forward (candidate comes forward and kneels)

Washing

(Blessing with holy water in silence and blesses the head and all the senses, putting two hands on the head of the candidate)

Priest: repeat after me

NOT MY WILL, O GOD, BUT YOUR WILL IN ME
NOT MY MIND, O GOD, BUT YOUR MIND IN ME
NOT MY SELF, O GOD, BUT YOUR SELF IN ME

(Sign of the cross is made on the candidates heart ☧)

Priest: AND IT IS SEALED

(Candidate rises and returns to the chair)

The Bidding

Priest: Let us ask God to pour forth the Blessings and Grace upon (name) who is called to the office of Deacon, so that he / she may faithfully and in truth guard the portal of God's Sanctuary, obtaining the reward of the saints and teachers who went before, which is selfless service in joy.

(The candidate stands with arms raised to heaven)

Priest: Let us pray

Priest: God the Father-
All: Pour forth Your Love

God the Son-
All: Pour forth Your Love

God the Holy Spirit-
All: Pour forth Your Love

Holy Mary, Mother of Light-
All: Pray with us

All Holy Angels and Archangels-
All: Pray with us

All Holy Orders of Blessed Spirits-
All: Pray with us

All Holy Ancestors and Prophets-
All: Pray with us

All Holy Apostles and Evangelists-
All: Pray with us

All Holy Disciples of Christ-
All: Pray with us

All Priests, Bishops and Confessors-
All: Pray with us

All Holy Teachers-
All: Pray with us

All Holy Saints and the Watchers of God-
All: Pray with us

We pray to you O Christ-
All: Holy One, hear our prayer

Priest: For your Church and all who serve within it, that they may
be filled with Truth and Love
All: Holy One, hear our prayer

Priest: For this chosen one ✠ that through the Indwelling of Your
Holy Spirit, he / she may fulfil his / her ministry
All: Holy One, hear our prayer

Priest: For the Healing of the earth and all Her children
All: Holy One, hear our prayer

Priest: Rejoicing in the fellowship of Holy Mary and all the Saints
and Angels, let us command ourselves and all our life unto Christ,
the Indwelling Light.
All: To you O God (candidate sits again)

The Ordination

Priest: Omnipotent Creator, Omnipresent Presence, sanctify ✠ (name).
Help and aid this soul to guard the Holy Sanctuary, to be concerned for
the Heavenly Hosts and faithfully assist at all your altars.

May the Will of Heaven rest upon this Deacon who perseveres in the
Capax Dei; the preparation of receiving God. Lay upon him / her the
Spirit of Wisdom and Understanding; the Spirit of counsel and
strength and the Spirit of Knowledge and Godliness.

Fill him / her with the Spirit of Awe and Wonder, through the increase of the Sevenfold Gift of Your Spirit. May he / she grow in Divine Knowledge, offering his / her life as a Holy and continual sacrifice unto You, O Great King of Love to Whom praise and adoration come, from all creatures of the earth and the Hosts of Angels.

All: Amen

(Candidate kneels with staff again, priest places his right hand on its head)

Priest: Receive the Holy Spirit - in Sevenfold Fullness in your surrender unto the Higher Will of Heaven and receive the office and responsibilities of the Deacon in the A.S.A. on the path of Christ.

(Priest binds the hands of the candidate with a cord around the staff)

Priest: Your lower will is bound by the Laws of Heaven. What you wish and will is secondary to your own life. Your animal nature shall be brought under the obedience and discipline of the Holy Spirit.

Here lies the promise within the Covenant, that you shall keep the sacred Teachings of Christ from this day on, until the day you leave this earth and body, going into the great beyond.

Will you keep this Covenant? What say you candidate?

Candidate: ....

(Cord is released from the staff and the candidate stands)

Priest: If you have understood these Laws, you will surely understand the wisdom of Daniel. Read from the Book of Daniel, and enlighten yourself.

Candidate reads: "Darius elevates Daniel to high office, exciting the jealousy of other officials. Knowing of Daniel's devotion to his God, his enemies trick the king into issuing an edict forbidding worship of any other god or man for a 30-day period. Daniel continues to pray three times a day to God towards Jerusalem; he is accused and King

Darius, forced by his own decree, throws Daniel into the lions' den. But God shuts up the mouths of the lions, and the next morning Darius rejoices to find him unharmed. The king casts Daniel's accusers into the lions' pit together with their wives and children to be instantly devoured, while he himself acknowledges Daniel's God as the One whose kingdom shall never be destroyed".

(Priest offers the tray with the relics and touches each of them with Holy Oil)

Priest: May Christ clothe you with the Garments of gladness and the vesture of joy and may they come to signify the fruit of your good works.
Always remember that the right use of silence is the first task of a guardian and host of the Most High.

Candidate: I will remain in stillness and speak when it is asked. The fruits of my labour are not mine to keep. I shall be at rest in the temple of Christ and await the Voice that teaches me.

Priest: (Book of the Scriptures is given)

Receive the authority to read the Epistles in God's Sanctuary and in every place where it is wished to hear. Open your mouth for the living and the dead and what you proclaim with your voice, believe in your heart.... What you believe in your heart, fulfil in your deeds.

Priest: In the Name of the Creator, Redeemer and Transforming Spirit ☥

All: Amen

Completion

Priest: (Name) you have received the office of Deacon in the Temple
of Christ, the Bride of God. You will minister at the Altar of Sacrifice,
which is the Throne of Grace, together with the Angels of Praise.

May the Blessing ✠ of God and the Hosts of Heaven descend upon
you from the hands of Christ, heal you, prepare you and provide you
with strength, joy and endurance for this Work that has just begun.
Amen.

All: Amen

(Holy Mass continuous)

Ordination of Priest

The mass is celebrated as usual. After the lighting of the candles the Deacon comes forward with an unlit candle which is then lit from the central altar candle or eternal flame. Deacon returns to its appointed seat.

Priest-Bishop: Almighty and everlasting God, the Fountain of all Holiness, by Whose Spirit the whole Church is governed and sanctified. Pour forth, we pray, Thy Grace upon Thy servant(s) who is about to be numbered amongst the priests of Thy Church and Holy Sanctuary on earth, so that with open minds and hearts they may receive Thy Blessing from on High, through Melchizedek and Christ, the Eternal High Priest and King.

All: Amen

Priest-Bishop: (addresses all)

Dearly beloved companions, now we all stand in the House of God, in this temple at the centre of the Universe. Here before the God of Hosts and the other celestial powers which we have called to be in our midst, we call before us (name) who would be ordained as a priest in the A.S.A. serving a life within Christ.

(Deacon rises and all say)

All: Adsum - I am present

(Guided forward the deacon kneels before bishop, while sponsor says)

Sponsor: Most reverend one and representative of the A.S.A. and the disciples of Arimathea; for the sake of this Church of Christ, we ask that you ordain this deacon(s) into the sweet but heavy burden of the priesthood.

Priest-Bishop: Do you know him / her to be worthy to grow further into the Light of Christ?

Sponsor: As far as human frailty permits one to know, this I know, and I affirm my faith that this soul is worthy to undertake the burden of this office.

All: Thanks be to God

(Deacon presents the candle to the bishop which is placed upon the altar. Mass continues until the Liturgy of the Word and Deacon withdraws to the appointed seat and reads the epistle)

Epistle & Gradual

Deacon: this is a reading from Ecclesiastes

I sought in mine heart to give myself unto wine, yet acquainting mine heart with wisdom; and to lay hold on folly, till I might see what was that good for the sons of men, which they should do under the heaven all the days of their life.

Then I saw that wisdom excels folly, as far as light excels darkness.

To every thing there is a season, and a time to every purpose under heaven:

A time to be born, and a time to die; a time to plant, and a time to pluck up that which is planted;

I have seen the travail, which God hath given to the sons of men to be exercised in it.

He hath made every thing beautiful in his time: also he hath set the world in their heart, so that no man can find out the work that God makes from the beginning to the end.

Then I looked on all the works that my hands had wrought, and
on the labour that I had laboured to do: and, behold, all was vanity
and vexation of spirit, and there was no profit under the Sun.

(Priest-Bishop performs Gradual & blessing of the Deacon)
(After the Gradual, the new priest reads the Gospel of the Mass)

Gospel of the Essenes

I speak to you.. Be still and Know I am God.
I spoke to you when you were born.
Be still and Know I am God.
I spoke to you at your first sight.
Be still Know I am God.
I spoke to you at your first word.
Be still Know I am God.
I spoke to you at your first thought.
Be still Know I am God.
I spoke to you at your first love.
Be still Know I am God.
I spoke to you at your first song.
Be still Know I am God.

I speak to you through the grass of the meadows.
Be still Know I am God.
I speak to you through the trees of the forests.
Be still Know I am God.
I speak to you through the valleys and the hills.
Be still Know I am God.
I speak to you through the Holy Mountains.
Be still Know I am God.
I speak to you through the rain and the snow.
Be still Know I am God.
I speak to you through the waves of the sea.
Be still Know I am God.
I speak to you through the dew of the morning.
Be still Know I am God.
I speak to you through the peace of the evening.
Be still Know I am God.

I speak to you through the splendour of the sun.
Be still Know I am God.
I speak to you through the brilliant stars.
Be still Know I am God.
I speak to you through the storm and the clouds.
Be still Know I am God.
I speak to you through the thunder and lightning.
Be still Know I am God
I speak to you through the mysterious rainbow.
Be still Know I am God.
I will speak to you when you are alone.
Be still Know I am God
I will speak to you through the Wisdom of the Ancients.
Be still Know I am God
I will speak to you at the end of time.
Be still Know I am God.
I will speak to you when you have seen my Angels.
Be still Know I am God.
I will speak to you tthroughout Eternity.
Be still Know I am God
I speak to you. Be still Know I am God. Thou art God-

(Priest-Bishop performs a short meditation / contemplation)

(Mass continues with the candidate presenting her / his own Credo)

Priest-Bishop: Brothers and sisters, companions, know that with
the help of Christ, this soul has chosen for the order of the
priesthood. This deacon(s) (name(s), has bowed its head before
this office on the Way of the small and narrow path. If anyone has
objections against this ordination, let that person speak now,
in the Name of the Most Holy One.

Priest-Bishop: This silence affirms the approval of the worldly
domain that surrounds this deacon

All: Amen - Let it be so in the days to come

Priest-Bishop: My beloved companion in Christ, it is now my part,
solemnly and for the last time to charge you how great are
the responsibilities of this office and how profound are its duties.
For it appertains to a priest to bless, anoint, absolve and baptize, but
above all, it is the awesome duty of a priest to offer sacrifice before
the Divine Throne on behalf of all humanity.

Wherefore, only after solemn premeditation and with great awe so
sublime an office be approached. Consider well all these things
before the irrevocable act shall be accomplished, which shall lay
upon you, the hand of heaven and the works and duties of those
inner worlds, laying the seed of Christ forever in thine soul with
this ordination of the priesthood.

Do you still wish to proceed with this blessed ceremony?

(Deacon answers)

Priest-Bishop: Strive ever to increase within yourself the fruits
of the Spirit, that you may be a bearer of God's Light, a Grail carrier
to the heart of humanity. Never forget how great is your privilege
to lift the heavy burden of sin and suffering from the world through
the grace of absolution, or to bring the little ones through the gate of
baptism into the Divine Protection. You whose duty it is to offer unto
God whatever is needed for Heaven's sake. With the Angels of
praise, adoration and prayer, let your words be a spiritual remedy,
your actions vessels of light, and let the aroma of your life be a sweet
incense in the church of Christ.

Will you, in the Name of the Most Holy One, receive the order of Priest?

Deacon: I will, so help me God

Priest-Bishop: Then may Christ vouchsafe to bring your will to
the perfection that is pleasing to God and strengthen you + in all
goodness, truth and beauty.

All: Amen

Priest-Bishop: Let us pray that the Almighty Living One in its Loving-Kindness will bestow plentiful Grace on this deacon(s), now about to be raised to the order of the priesthood.

(All kneel and the deacon(s) prostrates face down while the Litany is sung)

The Litany

God the Father seen of none,
God the creator the co-eternal Son,
God the Spirit with them One,
hear us Holy Trinity.

God Eternal Mighty King,
Unto Thee our love we bring,
Through Thy world the praises ring,
We are Thine O Trinity.

Christ the One of Life and Light,
Ruler of the starry height,
Fount of Glory Infinite,
Thee we worship Christos.

Mighty One we hail Thee here,
Recognize Thy Presence dear,
Feel and know that Thou art near,
Keeping thus Thy promise.

Though Thy face we cannot see,
As of old in Galilee,
Strong in faith we worship Thee,
Every present Christos.

From the Father we have heard,
Of the gifts Thy Hand conferred,
We have proved Thy Holy Word,
Be that Gift outpoured.

Though Thy form from earth hath gone,
Thine Apostles handed on,
Sacramental Benison,
Be that Blessed with us.

We this power would convey,
Strengthen Thou our hands we pray,
Pour Thy Might through us today,
Hear us Holy Christos.

Monarch at Thy Feet we kneel,
For Thy servant(s) we appeal,
Fill their hearts with Holy Zeal +
In Thy service Christos

Thou of Holy Church the head,
Mystic power upon them shed +
By Thy Love may they be led +
Hear us Holy Christos.

Link in mystic bond with Thee,
These Thy priests that they may be,
From the world bound they set free,
By Thy Power, Christos.

May they stand before Thy Face,
Filled with Love and Heavenly Grace,
Grant them with Thy Saints a Place,
Near Thee Anointed Christos.

(Bishop alone sings next three verses)

We beseech Thee, hear our prayer,
Bless + Thy servant prostrating here,
Hold them in Thy Loving care,
Hear us O Holy Trinity.

Hear Thy servants as they pray,
Help Thy chosen ones today,

Bless + and Hallow them for aye,
Hear us Holy Trinity

Pour Thy Lovingkindness great,
On each Thy chosen candidate,
Bless + Hallow and + Consecrate,
Hear us O Holy Trinity.

(all sing together)

God the Father, seen of none,
God the co-eternal Son,
God the Spirit, with them One,
We are Thine O Trinity.
Amen.

(Bishop helps candidate to rise and prays)

Priest-Bishop: O God of Hosts, Who has made me, Thy servant standing before you, an instrument of Thy Will, and a channel of Thy Power: now according to the Apostolic Succession of Arimathea that follows the Way of Christ, passed on in an unbroken line by the laying on of hands, I present to Thee this Thy servant (name) that (s)he may become Thy priest and a bridge between heaven and earth.

So look with favor upon Thy servant (name) who sits before the Throne of Thy Majesty, clothe this soul with the mantle of Thy priesthood, wherewith Thou didst adorn Thy faithful servants in ages past. Strengthen Thy servant, O Most Holy One, that this priest may ever serve Thee, by night and day, O Giver of All, Creator of Heaven and earth and Absolute One.

All: Amen

Priest-Bishop: O Christ, pour forth Thy Sanctifying Grace upon this Thy servant. May wisdom and understanding guide the life of this priest and may the beauty of Holiness adorn its life and work, so that in the duties of the priesthood, begun, continued and ended in Thee,

this priest presents the Abundance of Thy Power and Grace. All in
the Glorifying Power of Thy Name, O Great King of the Heart, to
Whom be praise from mankind and all Angels of Heaven.

All: Amen

(Bishop and all other priests present lay their hands upon the head
of the candidate)

Priest-Bishop: O Christ, Teacher of Humanity and Great Healer of
the soul, Whose strength lies in stillness and peace, grant that this
servant who is joined with us, will now dedicate its life unto you,
gathered in the sacred priesthood. May henceforth this priest,
minister faithfully your power and duties upon the earth, providing
the Will of the One-Who-is Openness.

All: Amen

Priest-Bishop: Let us pray that The Almighty Living One may
multiply the Gifts of the Spirit in these servants, for the work
of the priesthood.
(All sing the Veni Creator, the traditional invocation of the Holy Spirit)

Veni Creator

Come Thou Creator Spirit Blest,
In our souls take up Thy rest,
Come with Thy Grace and Heavenly Aid,
To fill the hearts which Thou hast made.

Great Paraclete, to Thee we cry,
O Highest Gift of God Most High,
O living Fount, O Fire, O Love,
And sweet anointing from above,

Thou in Thy Sevenfold Gift art known,
Thee Finger of God's Hand we own,
The promise of the Father, Thou,
Who dost the tongue with power endow.

Kindle our senses from above,
And make our hearts overflow with love,
With patience firm and virtue high,
The weakness of our flesh supply.

Far let us drive our tempting foe,
And thine abiding Peace bestow,
So shall we not with for guide,
Turn from the path of life aside,

May Thy Grace on us bestow,
The Father, and the Son to know,
Thee through endless time confessed,
Of both Eternal Spirit Blest.

All Glory while the ages run,
Be to the Father, and the Son,
Who gave us Life, the same to Thee,
O Holy Spirit, Eternally.

All: Amen

(Bishop again lays hands upon the head of the candidate)

Priest-Bishop: Receive the Holy Spirit for the office and work
of a priest in the Church and Temple of God. You whose sins
and trespasses are forgiven and absolved in this Holy Sanctuary,
and whose life is freed from the chains of ignorance.

(Hands of Bishop extended)...... O God, the Source of all Holiness from
Whom comes all true consecration and spiritual benediction, we pray
Thee to open + to Thy Heavenly Grace, the heart and mind of this
servant, who has been raised to the priesthood, that through this soul Thy
Power may abundantly flow for the service of humanity and all creation.

May this soul be truthful and ardent as a co-worker in our order and
so prove to be a worthy vehicle for the sacred charge reposed in
them. Through Thy spotless Blessing this soul shall change and
transform bread and wine into the Divine Body and Blood.

May this servant keep the vessel of their ministry pure and undefiled; may righteousness spring forth within this heart and be filled with compassion for the multitude that they forget themselves in service of others.
May the Radiance of Thy Glory and Love shine ever more brightly in this soul and priest before Thee, until, steadfast (s(he) rises to full spiritual maturity unto the measure and stature of Christ.
The Beloved One shall be embraced by the Lover in the Father, Son + and Holy Spirit.

(All are seated and the candidate receives the stole)
Priest-Bishop: Take upon you the yoke of Christ, signifying the submission of your personal will to that Perfect Will, which is in Heaven, and as a symbol of the power of this priestly office, which is the ever-flowing stream of Christ's Love.

(Bishop dressed candidate in chasuble)
Priest-Bishop: Be you now clad in the garment of the priesthood, symbolic of God's all-compassing Love, vested in it, you shall offer Christ's primordial sacrifice: that of the "Lamb slain from the foundation of the world".

(Bishop anoints the hands of the candidate with the oil of the Catechumens)
Priest-Bishop: Be pleased O God, to consecrate and hallow these hands by this anointing and + keep them, so that whoever they + bless, may be blessed, and whoever they hallow, may be sanctified and guarded against all assaults of evil, in the Name of our Great Teacher and Healer, Christ the Redeemer.

(The hands of the candidate are bound by a linen strip and Bishop delivers a chalice and paten to the new priest)

Priest-Bishop: In the Name of Christ, receive the authority to make sacrifice before God, to offer the Holy Eucharist or the Ritual of Yahushua, descending from the lineage of Melchizedek, both for the living and the dead, for all that is now, past and future.

(New priest says the following prayer. After this, the pectorial cross and priest ring are presented and put on)

Prayer of the priest

Help me O God to cast from me all iniquity, that I may enter with a pure mind into the Holy of Holies, through Christ the Immanent Light. Amen

May the Holy Ones, whose pupil I aspire to become, show me the light that I seek, give me the strong aid of their compassion and their wisdom.

There is a peace that passes understanding, it abides in the hearts of those who live in the Eternal.

There is a power that marks all things new, it lives and moves in those, who know the Self as One.

May that Peace brood over me, that power uplift me, till I stand where the One initiator is invoked, till I see His star shine forth. Amen

Priest-Bishop: Receive these Gifts O God on behalf of Thy priest (name) out of love for Whom we offer this Holy Sacrifice.

(From this moment on the deacon co-celebrates Mass now continuing with the Prayers of the Faithful)

(During the Canon of the Mass)

Priest-Bishop: And especially for him / her at this altar, whom in Christ's Holy Name, we have raised to the order of the priesthood this day.

(After the veneration of saints and before the fraction)

Priest-Bishop: Is it your will to abide in communion with me, as co-servant of the Apostolic lineage of Arimathea and the Way of Christ?

Candidate-Priest: It is my will to be in communion with you, for Divine service and worship

Priest-Bishop: Will you offer due reverence to the Teachings and to the Righteous Ones of this tradition?

Candidate-Priest: I will

Priest-Bishop: In God's Holy Name you are received and you are adopted in the priesthood of the A.S.A. and may the Power of + Christ illumine and abide with you always.

Candidate-Priest: And also with you

Priest-Bishop: Pray for me Brother / Sister

Candidate-Priest: May God reward you

Final address

Priest-Bishop: Reverend servants of God, I must warn you that what you have to handle is not without dangers. Therefore attend diligently to the sequence of the Holy Eucharist, especially to the consecration, the breaking and communion of the Host. May you also be careful in everything that appertains to the administration of the Sacraments of the Holy Church, that you adhere to the form set forth by lawful authority and revealed by the saints of God, do not presume to depart therefrom in any detail.

Consider attentively the Holy Order you have now taken and be ever mindful of the sacred trust that the Divine has now reposed in you, since it hath pleased God to call you thus closer to Itself, forget not the service of humanity, which is the Golden Pathway to the Glorious Presence. Freely you have received, now freely give.

(candidate addresses congregation)

Candidate: Hear you all present, seen and unseen. This soul (name) has been set apart, hallowed and consecrated for the work of the God of Hosts, in the office of Christ's Priesthood.

Priest-Bishop: (addresses priest)
Christ hath sworn and he shall not repent! You are now priest after
the Order of Melchizedek and the lineage of Christ of which the
A.S.A. is a pathway into the world. Follow in the footsteps of Christ,
the Eternal High Priest and King.

The Blessing of God Almighty, the Father +, the Son +, and the Holy
Spirit +, come down upon you, that you may be blessed in this
priestly order, offering the sacrifice unto the Divine, to Whom be
praise and adoration from mankind and the Angel Hosts forever.
Amen. Amen. Amen

All: Amen

(The Bishop and new priest conclude the Holy Mass with the fraction
and communion)

Ordination & Blessing of an Exorcist

A.S.A. APOSTOLIC SUCCESSION OF ARIMATHEA

During Mass on behalf of the candidate-Exorcist & this should be
a Votive Mass of St Dionysius the Areopagite. Mass begins until
Collect and prayer.

Priest-Bishop: (Collect & prayer)
Eternal God, Thou art the Ancient of Days, Who art the Creator of
all things visible and invisible, bestow Thy Spirit upon Thy priest,
(name), that s / he may be armed with righteousness. Confer upon her
/ him Thy Authority to banish evil spirits, heal, make whole and to
save that which has been lost. We ask this, oh Sovereign One of
the Spiritual Hosts Who reigns in Ineffable Glory forever, through
Christ, the Son of Light.

All: Amen

Epistle (liturgy of the Word)

Candidate: Gospel of Mark 1:24

And they went into Capernaum; and straightway on the Sabbath day
he entered into the synagogue and taught.
And they were astonished at his doctrine: for he taught them as one
who had authority, and not as the scribes did.

And there was in their synagogue a man with an unclean spirit; and
he cried out, saying: "Let us alone, what have we to do with thee,
thou Jesus of Nazareth? Art thou come to destroy us? I know thee,
who thou art, the Holy One of God."

And Jesus rebuked him, saying, 'Hold thy peace, and come out of him.'
And when the unclean spirit had torn him, and cried out with a loud
voice, he came out of him. …
And immediately The fame of Yahushua spread abroad and
throughout all of the region about Galilee.

(Priest-Bishop performs Gradual & second reading)

Mary of Magdala
".... And desire said, I did not see you descending, but now I see you
ascending. Why do you lie since you belong to me?
The soul answered and said, I saw you. You did not see me nor
recognize me. I served you as a garment and you did not know me.
When it said this, it (the soul) went away rejoicing greatly.

Again it came to the third power, which is called ignorance.

The power questioned the soul, saying, Where are you going?
In wickedness are you bound. But you are bound; do not judge!
And the soul said, Why do you judge me, although I have not judged?

I was bound, though I have not bound.

I was not recognized. But I have recognized that the All is being
dissolved, both the earthly things and the heavenly.

When the soul had overcome the third power, it went upwards
and saw the fourth power, which took seven forms.

The first form is darkness, the second desire, the third ignorance,
the fourth is the excitement of death, the fifth is the kingdom
of the flesh, the sixth is the foolish wisdom of flesh, the seventh
is the wrathful wisdom. These are the seven powers of wrath.

They asked the soul, whence do you come slayer of men, or where
are you going, conqueror of space?

The soul answered and said, what binds me has been slain, and what
turns me about has been overcome, and my desire has been ended,
and ignorance has died.

Prayer over the kneeling Priest

Priest-Bishop: Let us pray

Everlasting and Living God, You have ordained the ministry of Angels and humans in a wonderful order, mercifully grant that Your Holy Angels, who always do Your service in heaven, may, by Your appointment, support and defend us; especially the Guardian Angel whom You have appointed to protect n---, your priest, who now kneels before you. It is for him / her that we invoke the power and protection of Your Divine Name, Oh God: which causes hell to tremble; Whom the Angels and Archangels, the Virtues, Powers and Dominations adore; and which the Cherubim and Seraphim praise unceasingly, saying: 'Holy, Holy, Holy art Thou, the Eternal of Hosts.'

All: Amen

Veni Creator

Priest-Bishop: (Imposition of hands) Send down Thy Holy Spirit upon (name) Your priest, to protect and empower this soul in all exorcisms conducted in Thy Name.

All: Amen

Priest-Bishop: Blessed soul and priest of God, take thine Rosary and pray in the words that Yahushua has taught you (candidate kneels with rosary and prays the "our Father"

Finishing prayer

Oh God the Holy Spirit ....(Mass continues from prayers of the Faithful until after the Consecration and 'Thee we adore')

Consecration of the Exorcist's Cross

Priest-Bishop: Our help is in the name of the Most Holy One

All: Who hath made Heaven and earth

Priest-Bishop: O Holy One hear my voice

All: And let my cry come unto Thee

Priest-Bishop: Oh Christ within all the worlds, empower this sacred cross, that it may be a breastplate to deflect all evil, and a prism of Thy Redeeming Glory, O Thou Who reigns from the heavenly cross forever.

All: Amen

(Priest-Bishop chrisms the Exorcist's Sword and then consecrate it by touching the tip of the blade into the chalice, then deliver the Cross and Sword)

Spiritual Armouring

Priest-Bishop intones: Take upon you the Armour of Divine Light

(Empower aura around the crown-centre with the Chalice of Precious Blood)

Priest-Bishop: (+ on the Head) The Helmet of Salvation

All: Amen

Priest-Bishop: (+ Throat) The Sword of the Spirit

All: Amen

Priest-Bishop: (+ Heart) The Breastplate of Righteousness

All: Amen

Priest-Bishop: (+ navel & sacrum) The Shield of Faith

All: Amen

Priest-Bishop: (+ Feet) And the Gospel of Peace

All: Amen

Priest-Bishop: (Front and back) May Christ, the Indwelling Light
go + before you and follow + after you.

All: Amen

(Priest-Bishop gives candidate the blessed pectoral Cross)

Priest-Bishop: All Ye holy Ministers of Grace; the Archangels
Raphael, Michael, Gabriel and Uriel; Rulers of the four Pillars of
the Universe,
Riders upon the winds of Heaven; confer upon this Priest of God,
(name) the benefits of your protection and hold her / him inviolate
against the powers of evil.

Though s / he walk in the valley of the shadow of death, let not that
shadow fall upon her / his footsteps, but let the Supernal Light of the
Holy Trinity encompass this soul in the service of the Most Holy One.

All: Amen

Interrogation

Priest-Bishop: Who is the great enemy of the Will of God?

Candidate: It is fear and doubt, but in courage and faith lies
the return to the Will of the Holy One

Priest-Bishop: Where does the soul find shelter and support in dark times?

Candidate: In the inner Sanctuary of the heart, where the Immanence
of God dwells

Priest-Bishop: What is your greatest opponent as a warrior and general of God amongst the Hosts of Heaven?

Candidate: Loosing hope in the presence of evil and when being tempted, pride and arrogance will be my downfall

Priest-Bishop: What is the weapon of Christ when you are opposed by demons or the lords of darkness?

Candidate: It is the presence of Christ itself before which all demons tremble and before which the princes of evil bow their heads

Priest-Bishop: What is the keyword that you will pronounce to the possessed soul in order to make them receptible again to heaven and God?

Candidate: It is the word that Yahushua used when driving out evil in Mary Magdalena and in many others.... Emphatha....
Open Thyself!

Priest-Bishop: Will you promise that in your work as an exorcist your dominion will always remain with the Hosts of Heaven and the Divine Will of God?

Candidate: I submit to the unwavering will of heaven and to the unfailing presence of the Holy Spirit that breathes through all the worlds

Priest-Bishop: Receive the sign of the Cross on the inner eye of unity (Priest-Bishop touches the third eye of the candidate with cross)

In you, before you, behind you, on your right and left, above you and beneath you, in your coming and your going, and within all the ways of your life.... Here is the Blessing and Power of the Most Holy One. Now and forever more.

All: Amen

(Priest-Bishop gives special Aaronic Blessing with prelude "Oh God of Hosts" - making the Sign of the Cross thrice over the new Exorcist - using the sword, holding its hilt uppermost)

Candidate: I bow my head and heart to the Most High. I yield to God and Heaven and so I will conquer the evil and chaos in the world.

Priest-Bishop: Stand strong Priest! Be like the eye of the storm and let Christ be the Axis of Light.... (candidate is pushed and challenged to hold balance)

Priest-Bishop: My last question to you O exorcist within the lineage of the Apostolic Succession of Arimathea: "who is your most important patron saint in you duty as exorcist"?

Candidate: It is the Holy lady and Mother Mary who is the most pure and holy presence together with Christ. May She be with me in my coming and my going.

(Mass continues after the Affirmation "Thee we adore....")

Bishop gives Holy Communion to the new Exorcist first and then to the congregation and concludes the Holy Mass.

www.ingramcontent.com/pod-product-compliance
Lightning Source LLC
Chambersburg PA
CBHW082018150726
48196CB00073B/544